Enhancing the Professional Practice of Music Teachers

101 Tips that Principals Want Music Teachers to Know and Do

Paul G. Young

Published in Partnership with MENC:
The National Association for Music Education

ROWMAN & LITTLEFIELD PUBLISHERS, INC.
Lanham • New York • Toronto • Plymouth, UK

Published in the United States of America
by Rowman & Littlefield Education
A Division of Rowman & Littlefield Publishers, Inc.
A wholly owned subsidary of The Rowman & Littlefield Publishing Group, Inc.
4501 Forbes Boulevard, Suite 200, Lanham, Maryland 20706
www.rowmaneducation.com

Estover Road
Plymouth PL6 7PY
United Kingdom

British Library Cataloguing in Publication Information Available

Library of Congress Cataloging-in-Publication Data

Young, Paul G., 1950-
    Enhancing the professional practice of music teachers : 101 tips that principals want
music teachers to know and do / Paul G. Young.
        p. cm.
    "Published in partnership with MENC, the National Association for Music
Education."
    Includes bibliographical references.
    ISBN 978-1-60709-304-6 (cloth : alk. paper) — ISBN 978-1-60709-305-3 (pbk. :
alk. paper) — ISBN 978-1-60709-306-0 (electronic)
    1. School music—Instruction and study—United States. 2. Teaching—United States.
I. Title.
    MT1.Y63 2010
    780.71—dc22   2009026072

For all my past and present music teachers and particularly my wife Gertrude, who shares my life and passion for spreading a love of music to students everywhere.

To love what you do and feel that it matters—how could anything be more fun?

—Katharine Graham

Contents

~

Foreword

Common sense (n.): Sound practical sense; normal intelligence; judgment derived from experience rather than study.

This is a virtue that some educators never acquire. Fortunately, many music teachers acquire the trait early in their real-world experiences and add expertise throughout their careers. However, how can college or university professors assure that *all* prospective teachers enter the field with a dose of common sense?

This book can do just that. Novice and experienced music teachers alike can read these tips, share best practices, and develop the assets of common sense in their work with children, parents, other professionals, and their communities. Can every teacher find immediate relevance in each of these tips? Probably not. But if the underlying advice intertwined throughout this book is followed, one's life and effectiveness as a music educator will be greatly enhanced.

Paul Young's suggestions cover all aspects of our profession. The tips range from those that support practice, recruitment, and pedagogy to those that emphasize personal and professional growth. He leads the reader through many intriguing vignettes and case studies to which all teachers can immediately relate. But his first tip may be the key to all the others—Focus on Children. It is critical to being an effective music educator, and one *all* educators must never forget.

A very successful music educator and principal, Young possesses a passion for the arts and a far-reaching perspective on the profession. While president of the National Association of Elementary School Principals (NAESP), he championed the merits of a quality music education for every child in this nation and beyond. He challenged school leaders to use commonsense thinking and balance high-stakes testing and accountability requirements with arts opportunities and experiences for *every* child.

Do yourself, and most important, your students a favor. Take this book with you to school every day and try one of the tips. You will be amazed at the results you will achieve with just a little dose of common sense.

Edward J. Kvet, DME
Provost and Vice President for Academic Affairs
Loyola University
New Orleans

~

Preface

Even though I served nearly 20 years as an elementary school principal, I have always felt at home in the midst of music teachers. I've been a member of MENC: The National Association for Music Education since 1973. Music teachers have a special place in my heart. The skills I developed in the trenches teaching music and the lessons I learned from my music teachers were invaluable assets in the principalship. I have always worked through the trials and tribulations of any professional challenge with the eyes, ears, and sensitivity of a musician.

While I served as the president of the NAESP during the 2002–2003 school year, I traveled over 110,000 miles meeting and interacting with principals and educational leaders all over the United States. I spent a lot of time in airport bookstores reviewing titles and selecting books to read during my flights. Many of my favorites were practical, motivational, self-help books for those in the business world. I decided that I'd try my hand at developing a similar book for principals, and *You Have to Go to School—You're the Principal: 101 Tips to Make It Better for Your Students, Your Staff, and Yourself* was published in 2004.

Subsequent presentations of the tips and advice at state and national principal conferences were well received. Attendees appreciated the common-sense, practical advice that could be used in their jobs and the guidance and mentoring that could help them get a new or better job. So, it was natural to develop a similar book of advice to share with music teachers, practicing or aspiring.

I was one of those children who got turned on to learning and experiencing the world because of inspirational music teachers. This book was written to help all music teachers reach their fullest capacity and focus on developing relationships that turn students on to a life with music. Just as with principals, the presentations have helped numerous college students and practicing music teachers reflect, evaluate, reaffirm, and see their important role in the school through an important lens: that of a principal.

People gain strength from mentoring partnerships. They become a source of motivation. Everyone needs a relationship with another person where it is safe to share, vent, discuss tough situations, ask for help, and be nurtured with unconditional support and friendship. Through this book, I want music teachers and principals to connect and perceive the similarities of skills needed to do their jobs. Both positions have tremendous influence. Both groups need each other. Principals and music teachers have unique opportunities to inspire students to reach beyond themselves. They are leaders.

But not all principals share my background and perspective. They don't always understand or know how to appreciate or evaluate their music teachers. And likewise, not all music teachers understand their principals nor do they recognize or acknowledge the important role they themselves play in their schools. Music teachers have the power to transform schools, to make them extraordinarily wonderful learning environments for kids. In schools where principals and music teachers develop respect and trust and support each other, relationships flourish, programs grow, and kids develop skills and enjoy learning experiences that will forever influence their lives.

I intend for this book to be shared by music teachers and principals. It should be a textbook in every student teaching seminar or capstone class in music education programs. It provides insights into what music teachers should know and be able to do in the real world. It is a discussion starter for professional growth. Principals will appreciate knowing that their music teachers possess the skills and attitudes described in this book—and more—and that they have common sense in the way they display them every day.

~

About This Book

This book is for music teachers who want to improve their professional performance and set themselves apart from colleagues of any discipline in a school setting. If your desire is anything less than achieving the very best, you won't want this book.

There are books that address a wide range of research and theory about music education and others that focus on very specific aspects of the "how-to" of teaching. This book isn't like those. Regardless of whether you are considering a career in music education, entering the first year of teaching, or nearing the end of a distinguished tenure, these time-honored tips are meant to focus on commonsense qualities and standards of performance that are essential for success—everywhere. This advice is applicable to musicians in any setting. The tips are intended to affirm quality performance for experienced teachers and to guide, nurture, and support the novice. This book outlines what great music teachers do. It is a straightforward, easy read. Keep it with your favorite books. Read it from beginning to end, or focus on the tips of interest that might address a particular need. You can set this book down and come back to it time and again for encouragement, ideas, and affirmation of your choice to teach music.

Music teachers quickly learn that the real world is full of challenges, heartaches, and triumphs that were never discussed in their college preparatory programs. This book is intended to help you deal with that reality. Readers of this book will easily relate to the fictional stories embedded within many of the tips. It is beneficial to read about others' practical experiences and to learn from their achievements or mistakes. Many of the tips describe the big picture, yet, upon reflection, can be internalized and become actionable for unique individual settings.

Not every tip will be meaningful for or applicable to every teaching position. Some might be viewed as trivial, most should be informational, while still a few might seem controversial. The reader will identify connections and common elements within many. Regardless, the intent is to support continuous professional development, share insights, present ideas from a variety of angles for further discussion and sharing, and promote the highest possible levels of musical performance and enjoyment for students.

If you visit any school and informally ask students to identify their favorite teachers, they will do so with enthusiasm and ease. And if you ask them to identify their most effective teachers, the responses are usually very accurate. Kids know. Most of the time, the same teachers appear on both lists. What are those little things that kids' favorite and most effective teachers know how to do that others do not?

When high school students know their music director is effective, they'll recognize the influence and connections to their quality performing groups and music program. If they perceive otherwise, the program is doomed. The same for the high school experience in general. If the public perceives all their teachers to be the best in their field, the school will be considered to be great. Otherwise, their negative opinions will erode support. A school or a music program is only as good as its teachers! They are the key variable that determines top quality.

If teaching music were easy, everyone would want to do it. But like other teaching positions, it is complex and challenging. Only those who develop effective skills and perspectives can survive a 30-year career and enjoy it! What are the beliefs of effective music teachers? What guides their actions? What values do they possess? What obstacles are most common? What time and energies are necessary to fulfill expectations? What is important and unimportant in the scope of the bigger picture? Insights and answers to those questions can be gathered by observing those who are most effective. The tips in this book reflect those observations.

Teaching music can be compared to a religious calling. It becomes an intimate, personal experience. Effective music teachers are instilled with a passion to be the best. Anyone can read and learn about what music teachers should know and be able to do, but only the best will practice these tips and others garnered from master teachers and make them their own. Doing so is a proven method to achieve greatness and fulfill the talents you were given.

Audiences for This Book

This book is for anyone who wants to improve the quality of teachers and the art of teaching music in schools. It can be used to support a variety of professional development needs. It is written for anyone, but should be of particular interest to the following audiences:

- experienced pre-K–12 music teachers
- beginning pre-K–12 music teachers
- music program supervisors
- college or university music education majors
- college or university music education professors
- students considering a career in music education
- after-school program administrators and teachers
- parents of students considering a career in music education
- principals, superintendents, and boards of education
- piano teachers
- freelance musicians and private instructors
- community arts advocates.

Profession: a calling requiring specialized knowledge and often long and intensive academic preparation.
Job: a regular or hourly remunerative position.
From *Webster's Seventh New Collegiate Dictionary* (1967).

In Summary

Music teachers have the best jobs in schools. They are the masters of a powerful core subject that can become the hook that motivates students to discover things about themselves, grow, and develop in ways no other kinds of experiences can. People never tire of music. It has the power to affect emotions, inspire creativity, and make one smarter. No child should be left behind in any academic area. The study of music can create connections that make learning in all other content areas more meaningful and fun. That is an awesome opportunity and a critical responsibility for music teachers. They must be the best of the best. This book is intended to help you, your program, and your students become just that.

~

Acknowledgments

This book could not have been written without the encouragement, assistance, and support of many individuals. First, gratitude is extended to my past and present music teachers who have shaped my thinking, patiently helped me acquire skills I didn't think I could achieve, expanded my horizons, and served as mentors and role models. Although they are too numerous to mention by name, I have been blessed to have been taught by and worked with the best of music teachers from my first day of school at Bremen Elementary School through the Ohio University School of Music, and my professional work in the Fairfield Union Local, Northern Local, and Lancaster City School districts. I thank my first band director, Robert Trocchia, for his guidance and recommendation to choose the trombone; my college teacher, Robert D. Smith, who eventually taught me how to play it well; and my postretirement piano teacher, Marjorie Seeley, who assures me that some day I will learn to play it well. All of my music teachers have influenced my life in countless ways and are the inspiration for many of the tips within this book.

Second, I thank the generations of members of the Bremen (Ohio) United Methodist Church who fostered a love of singing and always encouraged my musical interests and aspirations. They unwittingly provided the performance venue that every aspiring musician needs. When I made mistakes, they reassured. When I succeeded, they applauded and provided the motivation and incentive to do more. They are the Bremen Town Musicians! My years with those faithful worshipers helped provide insights into the way music inspires vitality within a community as well as the music teacher's responsibilities in creating a high-quality musical life for all its learners.

Third, I am blessed with a wife, two daughters, and large family that love, appreciate, and value all kinds of music. My wife Gert, teaches vocal and instrumental music in the Lancaster City Schools in Lancaster, Ohio. My daughter Katie is the principal oboist with the Florida Symphony Orchestra in Tampa. My younger daughter Mary Ellen, a sales representative for Mc-Graw-Hill Higher Education, lives in Chicago with her husband Eric Rahn, and both are avid music lovers and supporters. Their unselfish sacrifices have provided me time to reflect, talk, share, write, and engage in a variety of professional leadership activities.

Lastly, my mother tried her best to be my first piano teacher, although I failed to listen. However, her passion for music and the lessons she taught a little boy inspired a young man to answer a calling and prepare for the most enjoyable of careers. She has been influential in all the tips and everything that I have been able to accomplish throughout my life.

Paul Young
Lancaster, Ohio

~

National Standards
for Music Education

No significant learning occurs without a significant relationship.

—Dr. James Comer

Relationships = Power and Respect
Relationships are often motivating factors in one's ability to attain success

1. Singing, alone and with others, a varied repertoire of music.
2. Performing on instruments, alone and with others, a varied repertoire of music.
3. Improvising melodies, variations, and accompaniments.
4. Composing and arranging music within specified guidelines.
5. Reading and notating music.
6. Listening to, analyzing, and describing music.
7. Evaluating music and music performances.
8. Understanding relationships between music, the other arts, and disciplines outside the arts.
9. Understanding music in relation to history and culture.

Source: Consortium of *National Arts Education Associations, National Standards for Arts Education: What Every Young American Should Know and Be Able to Do in the Arts* (Reston: VA: MENC, 1999).

~

PART I

TIPS THAT ESTABLISH EFFECTIVE PRACTICE WITH STUDENTS

Introduction

Like all educators, music teachers must continually work to build relationships with students that foster learning. Today's kids enter school with different experiences and needs than generations before them. As a result, the need to adapt professional practice and change with the times is ever-present in schools—and especially in the study of music.

When principals interview individuals to fill music positions, most would agree that they are looking for a candidate with a prerequisite, high-level competency in musical skills. The reality is, however, that not all principals have a suitable background to adequately assess musicality or technical skills. But the best do know how to ask a series of questions that probe the candidate's psychological health. The healthier the candidate is psychologically, the less they will appear to need to change. Those same individuals will also be the most competent and most capable of change.

The tips and advice in this section, and those that follow, are presented to help music educators teach to standards and promote change. For change to occur there has to be some rub. Some of the tips might rub the reader the wrong way. That is not all bad. They will prompt you to think. Take special note of advice that catches your eye, whether you agree totally or not, and reflect with respected and effective music educators. The dialogue and sharing of perspectives will result in continuous adult learning—the ultimate reward for reading this book.

Principals sometimes must remind some music teachers that their charge is to work with students in the "real world." A broad perspective is necessary, not a narrow focus. It's what principals want all teachers to possess. But some musicians have a difficult time adjusting to the realities of learning environments outside the insulated halls of the college or university school of music. Read this section and spend time reflecting and self-assessing your current professional performance or your level of preparation for entering the field. A self-assessment guide appears at the end of the section, as does one at the end of each section throughout the book. Music education students would be wise to utilize the guide before or during their student teaching experience. The guides are not intended to be all-inclusive lists of what you should know and be able to do. With your colleagues and teachers, brainstorm ideas about best practices, recommendations, advice, tips, hints, insights, and special skills that superstar music teachers have achieved and demonstrated for years.

Best wishes as you strive to become the best in your business.

Change is inevitable; growth is optional.

—Author Unknown

TIP 1

~

Focus on Children

Focusing on children should seem obvious, yet music teachers, like all educators, can use a reminder. Perhaps it is because the music itself is their first love that many music teachers sometimes forget to focus on their students' needs. No doubt, there can be enough reasons to narrow one's focus: a rush to prepare the high school chamber singers for the annual state contest, the need to assure the recruitment class participation rate is high, or an aspiration to achieve the highest standards. Consumed by their work, music teachers sometimes alienate themselves from students, parents, and professional colleagues by demanding that all life functions focus on the performing group and the task at hand, forgetting the individual needs and activities of individuals.

There is an old adage that goes something like this: "People might not always remember what you said or what you did, but they will remember how you made them feel." If students don't experience positive feelings about their musical experiences and their relationship with those who teach them, they may develop a negative attitude and a dislike for music that can affect them for a lifetime. No teacher wants to leave that legacy.

Remember, nothing is as important as the children teachers face in their classrooms. Make sure that every decision that is contemplated and ultimately made and each musical selection that is performed, studied, or created is made in the best interest of all students.

The teachers' best mirror is their students.

—Dr. Todd Whitaker, Indiana State University

TIP 2

~

Maintain Perspective

Don't expect young kids to perform what you did in college. And don't assume that each talented student will want to become a music major. Ever hear that advice before? Yet, repeatedly each year, there are too many beginning teachers who challenge their high school marching bands to perform favorite charts made popular by college bands. Whose ego is being fed? The results are often embarrassing, more so for the teacher than students. Many beginning teachers find themselves in small programs, sometimes with fewer than 30 players. It is unrealistic to think that such few performers can sound like a 200-piece college band.

There is nothing wrong with providing a challenge. It inspires motivation that can lead to excellence. Yet, most high school musicians haven't attained the performance maturity to handle the demands of works played by college ensembles. To assume that a group can or will is often an indication of an inappropriate perspective.

It is best to choose and perform musical selections that feature the strengths of each individual ensemble. It is much more admirable to perform music well, even though it may be easier, than to program works with demands that can never be met.

TIP 3

~

Expose Students to
All Genres of Music

Sally was a math teacher at Crestline Middle School, but she didn't like geometry. She didn't learn the concepts of geometry very well in college and subsequently developed a dislike for that part of mathematics. Sally began her career teaching low-track math classes, did just enough to get by, and stayed below the radar of her administrators. After her initial probationary period had expired, it became increasingly evident to her colleagues in the math department that her students were performing poorly in geometry. Once tenured, Sally brazenly told her colleagues that she didn't like geometry, didn't spend much time trying to teach key units, and didn't care what anyone thought. Year after year, students sat through Sally's math classes and moved on unprepared for higher level courses.

If a music teacher didn't like jazz, could that form of music be avoided? How about avant-garde styles or music of Middle Eastern cultures? Not in a high-quality music program. Yet, many students go through school lacking any introduction, training, review, or performance in specific genres. The most frequent excuse is a lack of instructional time, but there are some music teachers who tend to be like Sally. Some don't like a style or don't feel competent, while most are so preoccupied with the Friday night performance or the spring concert that they fail to expose their students to a broad spectrum of genres.

Most students can do little to avoid math teachers like Sally. But their music courses are often electives. They can opt out when things are bad.

Students and their parents recognize and expect high-quality music programs. A narrow curriculum excludes too much of what students need to learn. And unlike Sally, administrators can move untenured music teachers elsewhere if students elect not to enroll in their elective classes.

TIP 4

~

Not Everyone Wants
to Be a Music Major

David was a high school trombone player who excelled in everything that he did. He was a top scholar, athlete, and student leader—a quality student every teacher hopes to enroll in their program. His talent on the trombone was such that everything came easily to him. He had a strong sense of self-discipline and practiced regularly. However, by December of his senior year, David rebelled from the pressure his teacher had been placing on him to pursue a musical career, and he abruptly quit the band program and his study of trombone. David's choice to study mechanical engineering in college disappointed his music teacher. The teacher's pressure to consider music had become unrelenting, souring what had been a close relationship.

There are many multi-talented students in high school music programs just like David. Maintain a proper perspective when it comes time to helping them choose a college and a career. Music teachers' passion can sometimes blind them to what is best for others.

Everyone lost when helping David decide his future. He left high school with a negative opinion of his teacher and the study of music. He lost interest in the trombone and missed out on numerous opportunities for continued involvement in college, even while studying engineering. Unfortunately, it appeared that his teacher was responsible for creating an unfortunate experience that might influence David's musical interests for a lifetime.

David might not remember specifically what his music teacher said or did, but he'll never forget how he felt about his conflicting college and musical aspirations.

TIP 5

~

Teach Students How to Listen

Too often, music teachers don't spend enough time recording their students' rehearsals and performances and teaching them how to listen, reflect, and critique their performances. Some assume most everyone can hear, but do they know how to listen, especially to music?

Prepare some listening examples, good and bad, focusing on intonation, tone, attacks and cutoffs, vocal pairings, balance, ensemble, or style. Develop teaching strategies that enable you to later assess students' understanding of what they've heard. Talk with your students. Teach and empower them to talk with each other. Ask students about what they've heard within the community, and ask them to listen to their evaluations. Encourage them to use their musical vocabulary and higher thinking skills while synthesizing their learning and experiences.

Invite professional groups to perform for your students. Contact nearby colleges and universities and request available performers and ensembles. Take a field trip to hear the symphony orchestra. Students will see that music can be a living art form. After the performances, engage students in a reflective and critical analysis of what they heard.

And a residual benefit of your efforts will be the teaching of audience etiquette. Your lessons will help students learn not only how to listen but also how to be polite and respectful of the performers.

> Listening is an attitude, not a skill.
>
> —Anonymous

TIP 6

~

Create Independent Sight-readers

A famous music teacher once said, "If I can't sight-read it, no one else can play it!" That may be a rather pompous comment, but regardless, it says a lot about the importance of sightreading.

In order to create a community of lifelong music lovers, music teachers must ensure that their students learn to be independent sightreaders. It is a universal expectation that elementary students achieve proficiency in reading, likewise they should be able to read music. But many do not.

All too often, it is just the pianists, the most talented singers or instrumentalists, or the prospective music majors who become proficient sightreaders. But what about the student in general studies? Sight-reading unlocks the world of music and creates independent consumers. It is a critical skill. It should not be reserved for the elite.

There is too much emphasis on performances and rote preparation. Some music teachers accuse their vocal counterparts of producing significantly less independent sightreaders than their band or orchestra peers. Many competitions, contests, and festivals have sight-reading components, but still not all students are taught how to prepare. Things must change. Do we need high stakes testing to drive improvement?

Start slowly. Pick music with which students can achieve success. Incorporate a sight-reading segment in every lesson. Continually teach kids how to count and analyze rhythms. Just as one learns to read in elementary school, the best way to learn to sight-read music is to practice. Practice every day.

TIP 7

~

Encourage Solo
and Ensemble Participation

Participation in solo and ensemble competitions and festivals is an effective learning experience that helps middle school and high school students develop their musical skills and confidence. For many, it may be the first time to publicly perform a solo or participate in an independent, small ensemble. Make sure it is successful. The event should be a highlight of the academic year and a great motivator.

There are numerous additional benefits of solo and ensemble participation:

- exposure to good literature
- opportunities for students to work closely and independently with friends
- development of teamwork
- parent involvement
- community involvement
- learning to play with an accompanist
- development of refined listening skills
- self-evaluation skills
- increased maturity, self-confidence, and self-esteem for each participant
- opportunities for recognition and support.

Solo and ensemble preparation can require a huge investment of time and energy for the music teacher, so plan well in advance. First, establish an expectation of participation, and obtain parental support. Encourage the music boosters to cover expenses for those students who find the costs of music, private lessons, accompanists, and entry fees to be prohibitive. Select music from approved lists that provides a developmental learning challenge and can be mastered at a proficient level. Schedule multiple times to coach each participant for weeks in advance of the event. Make sure adequate numbers of accompanists are available who are experienced and capable of working with and supporting maturing students. Capitalize on the individual time with students to build rapport and increase their self-confidence.

Most teachers from other content areas would shudder if they were to subject themselves to review and public assessment of students like those who coach students for solo and ensemble events. But think how students' reading and math skills might improve if there were such a venue!

Attend a solo and ensemble event. Review the printed program of participants. Likely, those schools with the highest participation rates will realize a positive correlation with the quality of their music programs.

TIP 8

~

Teach Students to Conduct

Allow your students to do what you do. Let them practice and actually conduct performing groups. You may be providing the introductory lessons and the only training many of your community's small church-choir conductors will ever receive.

Before the end of high school, all students should understand and demonstrate the basics of conducting choral and instrumental groups. They need to know that conducting is a right-handed art. Work with them so that their hands don't mirror each other but rather work independently to provide cues and bring out the expressive parts of the music. Help them learn to start and stop music without counting out loud and to express the dynamics and nuances of music nonverbally.

It takes a considerable amount of confidence to stand in front of an audience of your peers and conduct, especially if it is something with which you have little familiarity. Likewise, it requires training to effectively lead a choral or instrumental group. Music majors obviously receive that training, but multitudes of laypeople keep music alive in places of worship and chamber settings as volunteer conductors. What they know and are capable of doing likely comes from their school or on-the-job experiences. Don't underestimate the importance of the time you devote to teaching conducting skills. Integrate your instruction during routine rehearsals by showing students how to analyze your movements and gestures. Let the entire performing group practice and imitate what you do. Only a few seconds are necessary. It will help build awareness and cohesiveness within your performing group.

Teach concert etiquette along with conducting. Instruct your students to applaud when conductors take the stage. Explain the standard process by which orchestral groups tune their instruments. Help students learn to become critical listeners and to express their appreciation in an acceptable manner. Teach them the meaning of the terms *bravo*, *brava*, and *encore*.

People often wonder what a conductor really does. Little kids love to watch and imitate them. But to be asked to accept responsibility and stand in front of a group of musicians as their leader can be an intimidating experience. Help prepare your students to take advantage of and enjoy those opportunities—and to succeed.

Special teachers make students feel special.

—Dr. Dale Lumpa, Englewood, Colorado

~

Teach Theory and History

"Can you tell me the value of a dotted quarter note?"
"What does the term *fortissimo* mean?"
"During what time in history did Wolfgang Amadeus Mozart live?"
"What can you tell me about Ludwig van Beethoven?"
"Can you describe any unique genres of American music?"

If you stood in the hallway of a typical American high school and randomly questioned students during a class change, you'd probably feel like the *Tonight Show's* former host Jay Leno reenacting his comedy routine on the streets of Hollywood. Even if you'd allow them more time, without the pressure of cameras running, most students would likely perform poorly on your informal quiz.

Could your music students identify and sing the songs of the U.S. armed forces? Do they know the words (and their meaning) of the national anthem? Would they be able recognize the name, sing, and discuss the origin of songs such as "Do-Re-Mi," "On Top of Old Smokey," "Take Me Out to the Ballgame," "Simple Gifts," "Swing Low, Sweet Chariot," and numerous others of our common heritage?

Music teachers must assure that *all* students leaving high school, not just those who have participated in performing groups, gain a comprehensive understanding of the elements of music. *All* students must learn how to listen to music, understand it, and appreciate it. The keyboard shouldn't be a strange object, familiar only to those who study piano. All students should be familiar with sounds made by the instruments of the orchestra, learn about an opera, understand contemporary music, and be familiar with a repertoire of classic American songs. The names of the world's outstanding composers should be as recognizable as any other famous artists, poets, writers, and actors in history books.

Work with your colleagues. Team-teaching a world history class from a musical perspective could bring it alive for *all* students in unique and creative ways. Don't allow educated students to move through your school system without a comprehensive understanding of music.

> There is always a moment in a child's life when the door opens and lets the future in.
>
> —Graham Greene

TIP 10

~

Teach Showmanship

Despite reports that draw attention to the negative effects of watching television, music teachers can use the medium to teach students about the features of good professional showmanship. There are countless examples of showmanship on television every day, both good and bad. Teachers need to help students understand the differences between those that are good and those that are not.

Watch a public television broadcast of an orchestra concert. Observe the professional live performances of a drum and bugle corps. If the performers make a mistake, they never acknowledge it in a way that brings attention to themselves. They learn to keep going with head held high. They exhibit confidence. Most observers never notice any errors. Kids need to incorporate this skill into their repertoire of performance skills.

Following the job interview and hiring process, William's new employer was complimentary of his display of confidence and personal presence. "Where did you acquire those skills?" the employer asked. "I'd have to give credit to my music teachers, I suppose." As they continued talking, he elaborated that they were most influential in teaching lessons such as:

- Someone will be watching every move you make
- Walk into the room with confidence like you own it
- Learn to be gracious with your bow, and melt the audience with your smile

- Always do your best. Don't let the situation or other people intimidate you
- Never let them see you sweat.

Life is a stage, and successful people learn how to take command. Learning to become a performer with high levels of showmanship skill is a distinct advantage of studying music.

TIP 11

~

Teach Career Opportunities

Sergei's father was unsupportive of his son's desire to pursue music composition in college. A high school junior, Sergei was bright and multi-talented, a potential valedictorian of his class. His father preferred that he study law or medicine, careers that he thought would provide considerably more security, benefits, comfort, and potential income. Their father-son relationship was deteriorating over the disagreement. Listening while Sergei described his frustrations and fears, pouring out his heart, Ms. Carter, his band director, offered to intervene on his behalf in a meeting with his father.

Ms. Carter compiled an impressive list of career opportunities and potential paths using the Internet, books, and professional resources. She collected short biographical summaries of famous composers who were "called" to music after unsuccessful attempts to appease parents in more high-profile fields of study. At the meeting, Sergei's father welcomed Ms. Carter and listened intently. He was surprised to learn of so many potential opportunities. With limited awareness, he assumed Sergei would have to support himself as a starving artist. He knew his son didn't want to become a teacher. He was unaware of the potential of structuring a program of advanced studies that would enable his son to pursue interests in several areas before determining a major.

Teaching music is likely the most visible career path with which people can identify. Sergei's father was surprised to learn his son could study composition and become an attorney with a focus in music business and industry. Nor did he know about the many opportunities in the film industry, music business, and retail, performance, or music therapy. With Ms. Carter's assistance, he discovered limitless career paths and opportunities.

Music teachers must advocate for their students in many ways. Sometimes, it may be necessary to take risks and intercede for their students. Help your students and their parents learn about postgraduate opportunities in many interrelated areas of advanced music study.

Self-Assessment Guide, Part I:
Establishing Effective Practice with Students

How to Use This Assessment Guide

Reflecting privately, or with the support of others, assess your current professional performance, or your preparation for the profession, along the continuum of responses provided in the chart (the numbered items correspond with the tips in the preceding section). There are no right answers; just be honest with yourself. When you are finished, your assessment might reveal needs and areas for further skill development.

You might also encourage a teacher, a friend, or a mentor to share with you how each perceives your professional work and compare and reflect together.

Informal self-assessment and evaluation are important endeavors for all professionals.

If you frequently engage in reflective activities, you should be well prepared for any outcomes of formal evaluation processes.

My preparation and/or professional performance skills indicate that I . . .	Strongly Disagree	Disagree	Neutral	Agree	Strongly Agree	No Opinion, No Response
1. always focus on children.						
2. Maintain perspective with regard to student ability.						
3. expose children to appropriate genres of music.						
4. understand when and how to encourage others to follow my career path.						
5. successfully teach listening skills.						
6. know how to teach and develop sight-reading skills.						
7. regularly participate in solo and ensemble events.						
8. provide students with opportunities to learn conducting skills.						
9. possess adequate knowledge to teach music theory and history.						
10. possess showmanship skills and know how to teach them to students.						
11. have adequate insights to introduce and teach students about a broad array of music career opportunities.						

PART II

TIPS THAT SUPPORT RECRUITMENT

How monotonous the sounds of the forest would be if the music came only from the top ten birds.

—Dan Bennett

To show a child what once delighted you, to find the child's delight added to your own—this is happiness.

—J. B. Priestly

~

Set Realistic Recruitment Goals and Collect Data

Good planning prior to implementing a recruitment program is essential for success. Working as a team, all those with direct responsibilities and eventual self-interests should establish recruitment objectives, goals, roles, responsibilities, and target participation rates. Without a solid plan, recruitment is no better than hit-or-miss. The life-changing commitments and decisions that students and parents must consider prior to becoming involved in a music program deserve more than a one-time sales pitch in a singular meeting forum.

Administer music aptitude tests. Review the results. Seek input about students' skill development and potential talent from elementary music teachers. Establish a priority list of students before the recruitment begins. Collect demographic data (e.g., student/parent names, addresses, homeroom, phone numbers, e-mail, etc.) and create a spreadsheet. Use technology and data-management programs. Collect information, continually update data, and streamline the collection processes by working smarter, not harder.

Set realistic targets and goals. Monitor participation rates. Reflect, re-think, and revise when needed to achieve continuous effectiveness of recruitment strategies.

Not all students learn to read at the same time, nor will they learn to sing or play a musical instrument at the same rate. Make accommodations for those who need them, both for the superstars and the strugglers. Make instrument switches when necessary. Keep parents informed of progress, and engage them to become partners in the learning process and in creating music.

TIP 13

~

Work Closely
with Classroom Teachers

Those best positioned to encourage and assist with the recruitment of young students, whether for band, choir, or orchestra, are regular classroom teachers. Their daily contact and credibility with students and parents gives them great influence over what students think and do. It is vital that music teachers enlist them as friends and allies in the recruitment process. The following suggestions can make this happen.

- Include classroom teachers in planning recruitment programs. They have strong opinions about the time of year to recruit and time of day to pull kids from class, how to motivate students, and the best methods to communicate with parents
- Make sure classroom teachers are informed in advance about all decisions and schedules
- Classroom teachers don't like to have kids miss instruction. Avoid excessive pullouts from the regular classroom. Teachers will like it best when 25 of 25 students are participating in your program—that is, with their *entire* class leaving all at the same time
- Ask the teachers to share positive testimonials with kids about their musical experiences
- Walk students back and forth from the classroom and your teaching area. Briefly provide the teacher with feedback and positive comments about student progress. Show appreciation to teachers for their cooperation and support

- Publicly express gratitude about classroom teachers' support at programs and concerts
- Reward teachers with personal favors for their support of your work and that of their students
- Seek assistance with hard-to-motivate students or those who need extra support
- Celebrate success. Invite the classroom teacher to share in the celebration.

Classroom teachers have the ability to identify groups of friends and student leaders whom others will follow. Adolescents are focused on their friends, and many times, recruitment of the leader will attract many followers.

A high-quality music program hinges on a successful recruitment program. Music participation is an elective and a costly investment for many people. Developing rapport and a personal connection with the classroom teacher is a key part of the success that results in a top-rate recruitment class. There are positive correlations with a huge potential for success when the connections between the music and classroom teachers, students and music teachers, and parents and music teachers are meaningful. There will be higher participation retention rates in beginning music programs when music teachers seek out the support of their colleagues.

And don't overlook the contributions and support that can be offered from elementary general music teachers.

TIP 14

~

Partner with the Local Music Dealers; Establish Expectations

Beginning band and orchestra students need access to new and used instruments and a quality rental or rent-to-purchase program. Depending on your community, that access may consist of multiple reputable suppliers, or few if any. Whatever the situation, dealing with music-store representatives can present numerous challenges and concerns for music teachers. They can also greatly impact the success of the recruitment program.

If your community has only one music store, representatives from that business will likely expect exclusive access to your school and recruitment of your students. But there could be other music store employees in nearby communities or the geographic area that also wish to canvas and supply your area. If there are two or more music stores in your area, they will be in competition with each other. American business has thrived on competition, so it likely can within your recruitment program as well. But expect a push for exclusive access.

Check with the school administration to review any policies or contractual agreements that may exist. If there are none, keep your principal aware of your interactions and dealings with music-store representatives.

Whatever your situation, set the expectations as you want them to be. If your district allows an exclusive contract with a local dealer, spell that out with all competitors. If you plan to do business with two or more enterprises, let each know your expectations. Make sure your students' parents are aware of your policies. Only recommend stores where representatives will know your program and provide top-quality service to your students.

During your recruitment meetings, invite store representatives to display instruments and make a short sales pitch. They may even provide instruments available for trial. But it is best for students and parents to visit the music stores of their choice, spend quality time trying various instruments, and consulting with and being "fitted" by an experienced salesperson before making a final decision.

Again, set expectations in writing when inviting music stores representatives to your school. Avoid playing favorites. Make your decisions for purchase and repair agreements based on sound business practices. Avoid anything that may appear to be a kickback or an unethical practice.

Many parents will be concerned about the costs of music instruments and might consider options of the lowest price, regardless of quality. Warn them of the potential issues of buying instruments sight unseen over the Internet. Also, warn parents of the possible inferior quality of instruments sold in larger discount stores. Most do not include repair agreements. And the old metal clarinet that has been passed through several generations of a family may have sentimental value but be extremely hard for a beginner to play.

Music-store personnel can become your best friends during time of great need. When the pads fall off your only bassoon the day before a performance, they can save the day with a loaner or fast repairs. Most all music store personnel are good, responsible people. Enjoy your professional relationships with them. Just make sure to establish the expectations of the relationship in advance so both of you know where you stand.

~

Create a Standing-Room-Only Recruitment Meeting

Word gets around in a community. Parents will arrange their schedules to attend school meetings if their children and friends are talking about it. Make sure your recruitment program is a must-see event!

Put into place what you know, as a good musician, to be the ingredients of a high-quality performance.

- Prepare an agenda or a program. Include names of teachers, phone numbers, and e-mail addresses. Don't spend valuable time reading aloud information that people can take home and study for themselves
- Display instruments, and have them played professionally
- Invite high school or college-age students who have previously been participants in the program to perform and espouse the benefits of music participation. Identify role models with whom young students can relate, and show them creating music
- Show videos or PowerPoint presentations that showcase your program's success and highlight performances
- Allow students to test the instruments and be fitted by professionals, and establish other times for that to take place as well
- Provide easy-to-understand information about instrument purchase, rental, or loan plans
- Acknowledge classroom teachers and administrators who attend the meeting

- Start and end on time. Entertain, teach, inform, motivate, and persuade.

Furthermore . . .

Showcase your superstars and former students. Kids want to be like those who are well-known and visible to them in other school activities, in the community, and who have made it big in the real world. Former students who have gone on to illustrious careers in music can make a huge impression on parents.

TIP 16

~

Recruitment Must Be Ongoing

Kathleen was a fifth-grade teacher specializing in math and science. She loved music and played clarinet throughout her college experience. She enthusiastically encouraged her fifth graders to participate in band.

In late January, a very bright student named Jessica moved to her school and joined her class. As Kathleen got to know her, she discovered the family owned a clarinet, but recruitment in her previous school wasn't scheduled to begin until grade six. Her parents were thrilled to learn fifth graders could start band at this school. So Kathleen sought out David, the beginning clarinet teacher, to tell him about what she thought would become a potential new student.

"Thanks for the information, Kathleen, but I don't see how I can start this girl now," said David. "I already have a class of six students with a semester head start on this girl. There is no way, no matter how bright she is, that she could keep up. I think she should wait until next year."

Kathleen had experienced this lack of flexibility before with David and the other instrumental teachers. She had wondered if he was uncooperative, uncaring, inflexible, or simply lazy. Perplexed by his lack of interest in Jessica' potential, she challenged with, "David, I am amazed! Here is this bright, promising student, and you seem to have no interest. What is it? I know you could find some time in your schedule that you could work with her. I think you should find a way to make it happen."

Still, David showed no signs of interest or agreement.

Kathleen continued with, "David, when a new student enrolls in this school, I can't refuse them in my classes. I have to make adjustments. Most of them time, they are way behind my other students. So I have to work with them before and after school and any other time I can make to help them catch up. With Jessica, she came working at least a year ahead of my students. I certainly can't just let her sit around and wait for the others to catch up to her. That's ludicrous. I have to extend the curriculum and meet her needs, just as I do all my students."

"But I've got seven other schools I teach in and no free time to come back and work with her." said David.

"What about right now?

"This is my lunch period. I'm not giving up my time to work with any child during my lunch."

"Then wait until next year, David. I doubt that she'll be interested then!"

"Sure she will, and she'll do much better when she has all the lessons in the sequential order," said David.

Kathleen turned and left the lounge, realizing that she'd lose her restraint if she continued talking with David. She clearly realized why the high school band program was in decline. There were never enough clarinet players to complement the rest of the band, and she clearly saw why. David had lost his passion for teaching and contributed nothing to the program. Kathleen could understand David's scheduling frustrations, the challenges of teaching in several different schools with inadequate instructional space, pressures of recruitment, and helping new students, but she couldn't tolerate his lack of interest and refusal to even meet Jessica.

Don't ever play the role of a David. If you see yourself in that role in a similar scenario, it is time to find something else to do.

~

Kids Don't Learn at the Same Rate

If every child entered kindergarten with the same capabilities, learned at the same rate, and progressed satisfactorily with his or her peers to the next grade, teaching would be much easier. But we are all different. Keep that in mind when a child first begins the study of an instrument, piano, voice, or any specific area of music study.

Gary's mother enrolled her son as a fifth-grade percussionist. A single parent, she had custody of Gary but struggled with the demands of the court-ordered shared parenting arrangement. Gary's father lived in another city and had visitation rights on Wednesdays and weekends. He wasn't always reliable picking up his son and had a history of violent behavior and substance abuse. He showed little affection for Gary or interest in his education. Gary had become used to being the pawn in his parents' stormy relationship. He lacked motivation and a positive self-concept and was performing far behind his peers in most academic areas. His mother had become accustomed to reports about her son's lethargic approach to learning. Because of her work schedule, she rarely made it home to pick Gary up from the childcare center before 6:00 p.m. But she'd read reports about the motivational powers of music, saved to rent a percussion kit, and hoped for a miracle.

Typically, Gary showed up for classes, but often didn't have his method book or drumsticks. Other students progressed, but he didn't appear to catch on, nor did his teacher think he cared. After a semester of classes, Stuart, his traditionalist percussion teacher, was considering asking him to drop out.

There are countless students like Gary in our schools. Sure, it would be great if they could show just a little enthusiasm, get organized and bring materials to class, act like they cared, and make minimal progress. But Gary's parents were never able to focus on those essential skills. They were busy fighting for their own survival. Gary was lost as he was shuffled back and forth. If he had potential, it would take a special teacher, with great patience, to discover it.

Stuart's traditionalist approach won't work with Gary. He needs special accommodations to learn to play percussion instruments and succeed just like many students need to wear glasses to be able to see. He needs a teacher who can recognize those needs, care, and make the necessary accommodations.

Now, fast forward the future about six years. During that time, Gary struggled to learn and keep up with his peers. He was never described as a stellar student. But he stayed with it. As a high school junior, he was playing in the marching band. His small group of band friends had become a positive peer group that kept him out of trouble and pulled him along to complete assignments in other subjects. Gary was becoming more outgoing and developing a sense of humor. He was happiest and proud when performing with the band. Fortunately, Gary had not been left behind when he was exhibiting difficulties in fifth grade.

Look around. There are Garys everywhere. Don't be guilty of leaving one behind because you couldn't change your instructional approach to meet individual needs.

Self-Assessment Guide, Part II:
Establishing Effective Practices That Support Recruitment

How to Use This Assessment Guide

Reflecting privately, or with the support of others, assess your current professional performance, or your preparation for the profession, along the continuum of responses provided in the chart (the numbered items correspond with the tips in the preceding section). There are no right answers; just be honest with yourself. When you are finished, your assessment might reveal needs and areas for further skill development.

You might also encourage a teacher, a friend, or a mentor to share with you how each perceives your professional work and compare and reflect together.

Informal self-assessment and evaluation are important endeavors for all professionals. If you frequently engage in reflective activities you should be well prepared for any outcomes of formal evaluation processes.

My preparation and/or professional performance skills indicate that I . . .	Strongly Disagree	Disagree	Neutral	Agree	Strongly Agree	No Opinion, No Response
12. establish goals and collect data.						
13. work closely with regular classroom teachers.						
14. develop mutual agreements and partnerships with music dealerships.						
15. create and conduct impressive and motivating recruitment meetings for students and parents.						
16. make allowances for and include those students who move to the school after the initial recruitment campaign.						
17. differentiate recruitment and instructional strategies to accommodate students' varied learning styles.						

PART III

~

TIPS THAT ENHANCE INSTRUCTION

I will teach things that are not in books. For instance, I believe that children will be better students if they like each other and themselves better.

—Ennis Cosby (son of Bill Cosby)

It is unreasonable to expect a child to listen to your advice and ignore your example.

—Author unknown

TIP 18

~

Refine Your Philosophy

"What is your philosophy of music education?" asked the director of human resources from an urban school district at Michelle's college job fair. Responding, she babbled for at least a minute, and while reflecting later, couldn't remember anything that she'd said. She was nervous and ill-prepared in her first interview. That question and many others had opened her eyes to the expectations and realities of life beyond the school of music.

What is your philosophy of music education? Is it built upon your personal observations and experiences or something you've read in books or learned in class? Does your philosophy distinguish between what should be learned and what should be experienced? Does it describe what you believe, how you teach, and that for which you might "fall on the sword"? Do you believe the study of music is necessary in a formal education? Do you believe music is a fundamental human need just like eating, drinking, breathing, or sleeping? Is music truly a universal language?

Michelle hadn't taken time to focus her thoughts about these questions and others like them. She hadn't written a personal philosophy. As a result, she babbled. The interviewer likely dismissed her in his mind before she got to the second question.

Expect this question about your educational philosophy, or one similar to it, in interviews. Whether you are an aspiring teacher or a veteran, having a concise answer to this question can be helpful. Keep your response short and to the point. Allow the interviewer to draw out more specific details with follow-up questions if he or she chooses.

Try philosophies like these. Tweak them to fit your personal style.

- I believe that all kids can learn. Because music is a basic human need and experience, all students should be involved in its study. Students who study music are exposed to opportunities that create a more well-rounded human being
- I believe the study of music can develop qualities such as self-discipline and cooperation. It can reinforce reading and math skills and a student's self-concept. Music study allows students to explore their inner selves and be creative in ways that very few other disciplines can
- I believe the study of music is an aesthetic experience that no child should be denied. Music is one of the life skills that sets human beings apart from every other form of life
- I believe an understanding and appreciation for music will have a positive impact on a child's ability to learn and feel in all other experiences throughout his or her life
- I believe a good education should develop the mind, body, and soul. The study of music can support development in those areas and much more.

Determine your philosophy of music education. It's extremely difficult to convey to others what you know and can do if you first don't establish what you believe.

Discussion Questions

1. How does one prepare and rehearse for a job interview?
2. What are some typical questions that should be anticipated?
3. Should one always accept the first offer received?
4. Is it a mistake to admit that you don't know the answer to something?
5. Do candidates with master's degrees have an advantage or disadvantage in job interviews?

TIP 19

~

Know What You Want and How You Are Going to Get There

Vision—one of the personal characteristics that allow some to move forward while others do not.

Shut your eyes. Imagine where you want to be in 5 or 10 years. If you still want to be in your current position, what do you want it to be like? What improvements do you want to make? What course offerings and participation rate would you consider ideal? What must you do to make that vision a reality?

Music teachers, like all leaders, must have a clear mission and a vision of what it is they do, how they do it, where they want to go, how they will get there, how they will bring others along, and how things will be better at the end. Without a clear destination, goals, a plan, and a map, people wander aimlessly and accomplish little. But even some who have a clear vision fail because they cannot communicate it clearly or help others see it for themselves.

Don't forget this key bit of advice. It makes good sense for the students in your classes, no matter their age, to know why they are learning each objective. Help them see the rationale and relevance and to always have a peek at the bigger picture that you see. You'll have to be persuasive and at times may feel redundant talking about your vision. Set clear goals, both short- and long-term. Talk about them with others. Post them on the wall. Let your goals guide everything you do.

If a task or activity doesn't have clear relevance to your instructional or professional goals, you should reevaluate why you are doing it.

Discussion Questions

1. What does a music teacher do if he or she finds that the principal lacks vision?
2. Or other colleagues in the music department?
3. Or the school administration or school board?
4. Or the community?

TIP 20

~

Teach for a Standing Ovation

Approach each class as if you were performing on stage in Carnegie Hall. As you reach the finale of each lesson, your students should be so excited about their learning that they will be motivated to stand and shout *bravo, brava,* or *encore!* Does that seem silly and unrealistic?

Read Scott McKain's book titled *All Business Is Show Business.* In it, he describes how today's children typically enter school having learned their ABCs by watching hours and hours of *Sesame Street* and other educational TV shows. They are accustomed to being entertained. Their attention spans have been shaped by television programmers that have conducted extensive research related to developmental learning styles of children. When material is presented in a manner that lacks flash and polish, the kids immediately tune out.

They do the same in school. And when classes are routinely boring, they begin to act out their frustrations in numerous inappropriate ways. Music teachers, because of their training and experience performing, should be among the most entertaining of all educators, but some don't get it. They present routine lessons without adequate preparation, in monotone voices, conveying little interest or enthusiasm. Their work becomes a mere job, not a passion. Because they present themselves as such bores, kids lose interest and drop their participation.

To catch the attention of today's young people, educators must be knowledgeable about what is being watched on television, video games, the Internet, and other media. They must understand how information is chunked

41

and how celebrities deliver it. The entertainment business is omnipresent. Every teacher should have lessons in acting. But acting is not about making everything funny. Not all movies are comedies. What music teachers can learn from the entertainment industry is how to entice listeners and connect with all learners. When students bond with their teacher, they become interested. When they relate, they become appreciative of the teacher's experience and what the teacher is doing for them. When students connect with their learning experiences, they want to repeat them over and over, and they want to stand and shout *bravo*!

T I P 21

~

Be the First at Each Rehearsal
and the Last to Leave

If you are responsible for a performing group, and you will be working with students after school or on weekends, make sure you are the first at school and the last to leave. Develop a communication system with parents that informs them of the time the school will be open and when students will be dismissed and should be picked up. Use weekly paper messages, telephone calling chains, e-mail, and Web sites to keep parents and students informed. Make sure parents have your schedule far enough in advance to plan their family commitments.

You could be negligent in your job performance if students are left alone at school, especially late at night without a ride home. Make sure you have assistance to ascertain that each student under your supervision is released to a legal parent or guardian. Make sure the music room or school is completely vacated and secured before you leave. Assign responsibilities if you have assistants or seek help from parent volunteers and chaperones. Nothing could be more damaging to your career than discovering two students had been hiding in a restroom and then vandalized the school after you left.

Music teachers must assume many responsibilities in lieu of school administrators when working with and supervising students in after-school activities. Plan with your superiors, and have them approve your guidelines. Inform parents of your procedures in a student-parent handbook, and have them sign that they have reviewed the document and are aware of your procedures and expectations. Never waiver from what you establish.

And if you are late for some unexpected reason, have an alternative plan that will immediately be able to be put into effect.

TIP 22

~

Start Class on Time

Too many teachers waste valuable instructional time at the beginning of each class period. Particularly at the middle and high school grades, where the level of socialization increases, students typically come to class chatting and continue unless the teacher clearly structures the transition and begins teaching or rehearsing within minutes of the sounding of a bell. It is easy to get distracted by students' questions and last-minute preparations, but it is inexcusable if the teacher is engaged in chatty conversation like the students.

Assign routine tasks such as recording attendance, distributing materials, passing out music, and setting up chairs and stands to reliable students. Distribute copies of important announcements or use e-mail and music department Web sites to keep students, parents, and the community informed of upcoming events. Limit the amount of time spent going over information many won't hear or remember.

Be consistent each day. Take control of the class. Teach the kids the routine you expect them to follow. Move things along as quickly as possible.

Returning to the band room from the staff lounge, Muhammad happened upon a student in the hallway who appeared to be experiencing a seizure. He immediately began providing assistance and helped move the student to the nurse's clinic. While still assisting the nurse, the bell rang and classes changed. Muhammad knew he would be late to the band rehearsal but realized his assistance with the student was desperately needed. After 15 minutes, he left for his rehearsal.

Approaching the band room, he heard his ensemble playing. He didn't think his assistant was on campus at this hour, and he was puzzled who would be conducting. He was pleasantly surprised when he stepped in the rehearsal room and saw Justin, the band president, in charge. He proudly watched for a couple minutes, and when Justin stopped, he thanked him for his assistance. "No problem, sir. We knew you'd appear from wherever you were sometime, but since you weren't here, we figured we'd start like we always do and rehearse by ourselves until you got here."

Muhammad fought back tears as his pride swelled for his students. His daily routine and structure had paid off. A positive work ethic had been learned and become an expected way of life for his students. He knew this was a moment he would never forget!

TIP 23

~

Stay within Established Times
for After-School Rehearsals

Bob hated the days when he left work early, rushed through heavy traffic, and arrived at his daughter's high school to pick her up from marching band rehearsal only to find the group on the practice field repeating their drills. He knew that rehearsals were scheduled from 2:45 until 5:00 p.m. Yet, too many times, the director needed to teach one more objective, review one more drill, or rehearse one more song. Bob thought the director appeared to be insensitive, lacked any awareness of punctuality, or cared little about others' schedules or commitments following rehearsal. To make matters worse, the director became indignant when students were not picked up on time.

Bob's car wouldn't start early one Saturday morning before a contest performance, and after quickly acquiring a neighbor's car and calling the band office, he was 15 minutes late dropping off his daughter for the 8:00 a.m. scheduled departure. Waiting inside the school, the director chastised his daughter in front of her peers for her tardiness. Once Bob learned this had happened, he scheduled a conference with the band director the following week. As might be expected, the band director didn't budge from the rule and necessity for all students' prompt arrival for scheduled departures. And he never acknowledged Bob's complaint about extended rehearsal times. Most of all, he never offered an apology for rudeness toward his daughter in front of others.

Parents talk. Chances are Bob later talked about his feelings with many others while waiting in the parking lot. Others would hear about his frustrations with extended rehearsal times and the callousness of the band director.

Like a snowball rolling down a hill, attitudes grow and gather force among others who also relate to the problem.

Everyone loses in a scenario such as this—especially the band director who needs to learn to look at his watch, show compassion and understanding, and practice what he preaches.

Discussion Questions

If informed about this scenario, what should the director's principal do?

1. Discuss some positive responses from the principal.
2. Discuss negative responses.
3. What would you do if you worked with the director (e.g., as an assistant) and witnessed this scenario?

Further Advice

If you have the slightest inclination that something happened in a class or experienced an interaction with a student or parent that might lead to a call to the principal's office, be sure to inform the principal before you leave for the day. Drop a note. An effective principal is better prepared to support you if he or she has heard your side of an issue first and will appreciate the heads-up.

~

Plan Ahead (It's Not the Kids' Fault That It Rained All Week)

East of the Mississippi River and elsewhere, marching band directors know the angst caused by rainy weather. When it rains in the fall, it seems it occurs Monday through Thursday, but the sun shines brightly on Friday in time for the high school football game. And the spectators expect to see a new show from the marching band, forgetting that it might have rained all week.

Experienced and effective band directors anticipate this scenario and others that rob them of valued rehearsal time and impact a performance. They learn how to teach the drill of a show in various inside locations—the band room, hallways, auditoriums, gymnasiums, classrooms—anywhere it is dry. They also know never to waste a minute when the weather is nice and always prepare a show well in advance. They plan for injuries, sickness, and personal tragedies. They are always ready, prepared, and appreciative of every opportunity to perform.

It is a measure of good teaching to be able to persevere through unexpected situations. It's not the kids' fault that it rains. Keep a positive outlook and help them rise to every occasion. It's that attitude that builds grit and character that will last a lifetime.

An attitude is nothing more than a habit of thought.

—John Maxwell

TIP 25

~

Speed Kills

Teenage instrumentalists want to perform every technical challenge they encounter as fast as they can. Seems they also want to do the same behind the wheel of a car. Teach them to slow down in both settings. Speed kills and leads to more mistakes. Technique doesn't improve when an individual or group plays faster or louder.

But learning this concept requires discipline. Private teachers work to develop it lesson after lesson. They utilize a metronome or audibly tap a steady beat for their students. Band, orchestra, and choir directors must do the same.

Arthur's middle school band played with amazing technique. Colleagues would visit and observe his rehearsals hoping to better understand his methods and collect ideas. They soon learned that Arthur's students were from a middle-class community. They didn't exhibit any extraordinary characteristics. Arthur's band room was small and conditions were crowded. Arthur left an unassuming first impression with all the observers. So what was his secret?

Arthur walked and moved about as if he were in a perpetual *adagio* tempo. He didn't rush. If anything, people would describe him as slow. But this steady and consistent approach enabled his beginning and emerging bands to play precise rhythms and technical passages more cohesively than most. He selected appropriate rehearsal speeds at which his students could master difficult passages when first learning new music. He helped them avoid frustration. Then, when they played accurately as an ensemble, he pushed the tempi forward. His approach took no longer than others. It achieved much better results. It is a best practice that every music teacher must learn.

Recommended for Further Reading

Researchers are producing remarkably consistent findings citing that elite status in most any endeavor is attained only through an enormous amount of hard work over many years. And not just any hard work, but work of a particular type that's demanding and painful. Citing the "Rule of 10,000 Hours," researchers explain that best people in any field are those who devote the most hours to "deliberate practice." It's activity that's explicitly intended to improve performance, that reaches for objectives just beyond one's level of competence, provides feedback on results, and involves high levels of repetition.

Elite musicians know all about deliberate practice. You can learn more about the fascinating studies related to the "Rule of 10,000 Hours" in *Outliers* (2008) by Malcolm Gladwell and *Talent Is Overrated: What Really Separates World-Class Performers from Everybody Else* (2008) by Geoff Colwin.

TIP 26

~

You Want Students to Respect You More Than Like You

It's a desire and sometimes a dilemma. Beginning teachers desperately want to be liked by their students. Those leaving college in their early 20s often find themselves having more things in common with their high school students than their elder colleagues. To be liked, they sometimes make decisions and engage in behaviors that can be compromising and dangerous. When that happens, they find themselves with hard-to-handle and disrespectful students and a less-than-glowing professional evaluation.

Sage advice from veteran teachers sometimes sounds like this, "Never let them see you smile until at least Thanksgiving." That may be extreme. But what those veterans really mean to convey is that it is much easier to relax your grip on the reins than it is to pull them back once you've allowed students too much freedom.

Insist that students address you with a professional salutation. Show them respect as well. Avoid humor that belittles another student or person. It is always best to be the butt of a joke, to have people laughing with you or at you but not at others. Be consistent, fair, honest, and always tell the truth.

Think of your favorite teachers. At the time, you might have seen them as intimidating. Maybe you didn't like them much. But for many reasons, you eventually came to respect them, and almost always, those you respected most you also loved.

Listen as the most revered teachers are described. People will first talk about why they respect them, their high standards, expectations, methodologies, empathy, patience, or compassion. The higher the level of respect being described, the more you can feel the love.

Discussion Questions

1. What are some of the little things, perhaps referred to as tricks of the trade, that you have observed masters teachers doing to effectively manage students.
2. How do they get results if the students show lack of discipline elsewhere in the school?
3. What are some of the temptations that challenge music teachers' ability to be consistent and fair?
4. Is there ever an appropriate time to tell a "white lie"?
5. How do you describe respect between you and your principal?
6. What must you do to earn your principal's respect?
7. What must your principal do to earn your respect?

The only way to teach respect is to model it.

—Dr. Todd Whitaker, Indiana State University

TIP 27

~

Be a Master Motivator

Can music teachers learn to be master motivators as well as excellent instructional leaders? Yes, everyone can develop their personal characteristics and exceed expectations. What follows are some motives, values, and observable actions that are shared by all master music teachers.

- Be generous with your praise of others
- Make sure your integrity is above reproach
- Expect the best and work continuously to achieve positive results
- Maintain your musical skills so they are second to none
- Continuously establish clear and achievable goals
- Look for others' strengths and good qualities instead of focusing on their weaknesses
- Keep an open mind, and be willing to change
- Have a vision of what you hope to achieve and make sure that others can see themselves in that same future. Get out front, and pull others with you rather than pushing them. Make sure you have purpose and direction in everything you do
- Listen to people, and actually hear what they say
- Provide caring, sincere, and confident feedback. Mean what you say! Don't be two-faced
- Cooperate and collaborate with others
- Ask questions and clarify what you don't understand

- Show people that you have a genuine, warm personality and that you care
- Demonstrate continuous energy and vitality
- Show enthusiasm for learning and mastering new skills
- Become an articulate speaker and writer
- Practice what you preach. Set a personal example that will attract others who want to work hard, achieve excellence, exceed your goals, and surpass their own possibilities.

Don't complain that students lack motivation. If that's what you think, take a long look in the mirror and determine if the reflection you see is of a person you would be excited to follow. If not, you've got some changing to do. Remember, everyone can improve their skills and learn to motivate others. Those who do it best are continuously working to find ways to be even better.

Reflective Questions

1. What motivational skills would others say you possess?
2. How can you develop improved motivational skills?
3. Who do you look to as a model of motivation?

TIP 28

~

Teach Students to Be Competitive and Accountable

Go to a middle-level solo and ensemble contest, get a good seat in the gathering area, and observe the students as their ratings are posted. Most often, those who achieve the highest rating scream and cheer while those with lesser ratings display a variety of unhappy emotions and disappointing behaviors. After a while, it's easy to identify the students from schools where they have been properly prepared for any outcome. They don't scream and cheer at the expense of others, and if they don't achieve the highest rating, they accept the results, act responsibly, and refrain from blaming the adjudicator. The final rating is not a surprise or shock but more an affirmation of their musical progress.

Effective music teachers coach their students to evaluate their personal performance against established standards. They prepare students using the contest assessment sheet as a teaching tool. Technical strengths and weaknesses are identified as well as the concepts of tone production, intonation, rhythmic accuracy, musical style, and interpretation. Their students clearly understand how they must perform according to preestablished criteria and learn to compare themselves against the standard and not another performer. The students understand that they are competing against their own abilities. Those who have been adequately coached carry themselves with confidence and dignity and are much less likely to act foolishly when the ratings are posted.

Competition can be healthy and an internal motivator that drives musicians to achieve great performances. But it can also be destructive and crush a student's interest and spirit. Competition is not solely about winners and losers. Teach students to do their best, critically self-assess their performances against high standards, become accountable for what they do, and accept the results with dignity and grace.

TIP 29

~

Remove Stereotypes

Research, some of it controversial, alludes that there are distinct abilities and attributes between boys and girls. Some researchers say, given a choice, that little boys will naturally gravitate toward toy trucks while girls prefer soft, cuddly dolls. Whether or not that is really the case, societal norms and values do heavily influence what kids play with, what we watch on television, read, wear, eat, drive, and on and on. Should the same be true of what instruments boys and girls select and eventually learn to play?

There are commonly known stereotypes impacting instruments and the sexes, and music teachers should do whatever they can to remove them. Boys *can* play the flute, and girls *can* play the tuba. Boys *can* sing just as well as girls. But teenage peer pressure can be brutal. It's not so much about whether boys or girls can capably play certain instruments but more about whether it is "cool" to do so.

Show your students examples of famous people and celebrities who play instruments and enjoy musical careers. Play video clips of women conductors such as Joanne Faletta and Marin Alsop. Feature boys dancing and moving in general music classes and school plays. There are countless materials and ideas available from music suppliers, stores, and professional associations. But the best way to counteract students' "genderizing" of instruments is to provide testimonials and personal contact with older students and adults who have earned respect within the community. Let students see and hear for themselves the realities and passion individuals possess for their chosen instruments. But if the male flute player you bring to speak to students is viewed as a sissy, don't expect changes.

Encourage diversity and expect adversity. Challenge the status-quo thinking, you say? Yes, particularly on this issue. Create an environment within your program that promotes involvement of all students, freedom of choice, and acceptance of differences.

And don't be guilty of having encouraged the next Jean-Pierre Rampal to play a tuba.

TIP 30

~

Take Charge of Your Schedule

For most principals, especially those who lead elementary schools, the annual development of the resource schedule is an odious task sure to bring complaints from teachers. Many try to alleviate problems and conflicts by seeking input and forming committees charged with creating the schedule. Others simply delegate total responsibility to a willing individual or small group. Many teachers' complaints are selfishly motivated, as they view the time their students are attending music, art, physical education, and library classes as "free" time. And they go about seeking free time and the ideal daily structure without regard to how their desires might impact others. It is wise that the music teacher work closely with the principal or scheduling committee to assure that classroom teachers' wishes don't result in the "schedule from hell" for the resource personnel. Many teachers volunteer to create the schedule themselves.

Every school is unique in its physical layout, number of classrooms and grade level units, preferences, and student/staff needs. Some include dedicated music rooms. In others, music teachers must move their materials from room to room on carts or other portable equipment. This takes time and effort. No matter the setup, you must plan and consider all that must take place between classes when developing a master schedule. It is foolish (and physically draining) to expect a music teacher to teach a kindergarten class on the first floor, then move upstairs to teach a third-grade class, only to return to the first to teach another kindergarten class. Arrange your schedule of classes by grade level or proximity. Help yourself minimize planning as well as make the most of your daily organization by creating a schedule that works best for you. Every teacher may not be happy, but the complainers likely never have been or ever will be. If necessary, develop a tough shoulder, speak up, and insist on what is best.

Teaching from a cart, meeting classes in overcrowded settings, or serving the ongoing needs of students in a very small school where a full-time staffed music teacher is unrealistic requires flexibility and creativity. If needed, use time before and after school for planning and preparation and meet individuals or small groups during your scheduled planning time, lunch, or recess periods.

No matter how well you prepare, things will happen that impact the school's (and your) daily schedule. Be flexible. Help others cope and adjust with the unexpected change. Make up classes when you can. When you consider the small number of times you will meet each class throughout the year, you can't afford to miss many. Work with the staff, be a team player, and always focus on what is best for kids.

Furthermore

1. Keep the principal informed about your special scheduling needs if you travel between schools.
2. Develop a special schedule for use when school is delayed or special assemblies have monopolized a portion of the day. You can't afford not to meet all your classes every day.
3. When developing a schedule, always allow instructional or student issues to affect outcomes, never the specific personality needs or wants of adults.

TIP 31

~

Learn Everyone's Name

It is quite likely that a typical music teacher could meet with as many as 500 or more students each week. It takes some special skills to become familiar with each of them and to be capable of placing names with faces. And extending beyond each student are parents, grandparents, friends, and neighbors. You have to know them all.

Teachers quickly experience informal encounters where their students point you out to their parents in the store or other public settings. Your skill in being able to recall names and make associations without warning can score big points with parents. Work at it. Memorize lists. Acquire pictures and old yearbooks and study them. Learn to ask some standard questions about a student's home or their extended family members, and talk about interests outside school. Show that you care. Praise works wonders. If you willingly devote time and interest to informal conversations, parents will tell their friends how nice and genuine you are. Be evasive, and they'll describe how remote and distant you appeared to be.

The key to building relationships is in knowing and remembering names. A name creates an identity, and with it are countless associations and experiences. Effective music teachers learn to live a life of building relationships, the key to opening minds. It is an act that is arguably more important, with longer-lasting results, perhaps, than that of conveying knowledge. Research shows that students perform better in settings where they sense they are welcomed, belong, have friends, and feel their teachers care. Knowing a name acknowledges another's worth. Knowing a name and all that is associated with it is more important than knowing just an ID number or test score. The key to working with people—and to long-lasting success—is in knowing names.

Some Tricks of the Trade

1. When you are introduced to someone, repeat his or her name aloud. It helps you focus and file the name in your memory.
2. Look for unique personal characteristics in others that help associate names with faces.
3. Study lists of students and parents in advance, and make connections when acquaintances are made.
4. When your memory fails, smile and look the other person in the eye. If your relationship will allow it, cover with "hey friend," "hey buddy," or some other familial statement.
5. Quite often, if used effectively, humor can get you out of sticky situations. "Greetings, Mr. Blue Eyes," or some other flattering distracter, can help bypass your temporary memory loss regarding a name.

~

Learn How to Treat Students Fairly

What does it mean to treat students fairly? Ask that question to most people, and a frequent response will likely center on treating people the same. But can effective music teachers really treat all their students the same? Not likely. Instead, it is better to be just in your actions, look at what each individual needs and requires, and interact in an appropriate manner. Parents know that each of their children have different needs and that one discipline plan does not work for all. The same is true in the classroom.

We make a big mistake in education by compensating everyone called "teacher" on the same salary schedule. Music teachers arguably work longer hours, have greater influence, and contribute more to the community than most of their colleagues. Music education positions are unique. Why should a music educator's salary be equal to that of a colleague who never works past the minimum workday? Is equal really fair? Hardly, but unfortunately the majority allows the status quo to continue.

Jamal was struggling with efforts to motivate a group of five fourth-grade boys in his general music class. They frequently became disruptive and acted out in ways that were inappropriate. Jamal had consulted with his principal, and he recommended several interventions. Furthermore, the principal told the students that if their behavior didn't improve, they could all face a suspension from school.

That bothered Jamal because he recognized that three of the boys were followers. He knew the two ringleaders had already been suspended several days and upon their return to school had been overheard to say how much they enjoyed being home where they didn't have to do anything. He didn't think it was right that all five could be suspended for the class disruptions, and he felt trapped trying to help the boys and avoid further involvement of the principal.

In this scenario, Jamal knew the same punishment wouldn't be appropriate for each student. But the norm in too many schools is to treat students fairly by disciplining them the same. Jamal knew that each boy had unique needs and home environments that were impacting their ability to stay focused and on task during class. To him, a last resort disciplinary suspension did not seem fair or just. He also felt the pressure from the students and teachers who were watching to see how he would deal with the boys.

Teachers at all levels must deal with the issues of fairness, equality, and just actions. Take time to think through the ramifications of your rules, expectations, values, and core beliefs. Talk about your policies, thinking process, and actions with colleagues. Schedule informational meetings with students and parents during which you address how you may need to handle situations *differently* in order to be fair and just toward all.

Another Way of Looking at Fairness

If everyone were required to take tests exactly the same way, then all students would need to wear glasses or none wear them at all. How unfair would that be?

We make accommodations to allow all students to gain clear vision.

We make modifications when it is necessary to improve conditions that make learning more suitable for individuals or groups.

We level the playing field and make accommodations in attempts to create fairness.

TIP 33

~

Be on the Lookout for Bullies

Bullying can be a perpetual problem in schools, particularly in settings where the structure is relaxed or direct adult supervision is limited. Bullies are un-compassionate and insecure individuals who stoke their egos and fulfill their needs at the expense of others. Don't be naïve—there are bullies in the best of music classes and performance groups. They may be subtle, but they are there. They are the elite performers who belittle the third clarinetists. They knock others out of the way to secure the back seats on bus trips. They domi-nate a clique or peer group and find devious ways to get others to conform to their behaviors, attitudes, and interactions. Bullies exist in every setting. You'll even encounter bullies among your professional colleagues.

There is a lot to be said about teaching kids to solve their own problems, but you also have to know when to intervene to settle disputes and disagree-ments. The pain of being bullied can become a living nightmare. The quiet and withdrawn child or the student who loses interest in the violin could be subjected to a constant harangue from his classmates. Bullies pick fun at the way others look, dress, talk, walk, act, what they do, their interests, and a myriad of other personal qualities. They may become aggressive or the bul-lying can occur simply in the form of a look, a passing comment, teasing, or simply by ignoring another.

Don't expect bullying to be solved by the principal or support staff in the front office. It is a schoolwide issue that must be addressed by all staff. When you detect bullying, pull the students involved aside and intervene. If a sig-nificant number of students are affected, hold a class meeting, confront the issue, discuss the problem in a respectful manner, and work to build cohesiveness. Stay neutral, and don't over react. Don't allow the problem to escalate. Reaffirm your positive behavior expectations. Inform parents of the aggressor and the victim, document your efforts, and make sure the principal is aware of what has happened and how you dealt with it.

Bullying can weaken or destroy the camaraderie of a performing group. It also creates anxiety and fear among victims that can impact physical and emotional health, making your class, rehearsal, or after school activity a time of day the victim may wish to avoid. Become an agent of change. Continually observe the interactions between your students, and work to create a climate that enables students to learn and develop positive social relationships.

Discussion Questions

1. What effective strategies have you observed that reduce bullying?
2. How can you confront bullies without publicly embarrassing them?
3. What are some emotional needs of bullies?
4. What can teachers do to address these needs in a positive way?
5. What should you do if a colleague you work with is a bully?

TIP 34

~

Limit Your "Okays"

Joellen stopped the rehearsal of *The Sound of Music* to make a few corrections. She was directing the orchestra and attempting to pull together the staging, singers, actors, and overall production during the first rehearsal with the orchestra. This was the orchestra's first time to rehearse with the entire musical cast. Her colleague and friend, Jeff, was responsible for the overall production.

"Let's make sure to watch each other at measure 51 so that we can observe the *ritard* and then resume at a little faster tempo. Okay?"

"I need to hear less of the strings and more of the solo voice at measure 24. Okay?"

"Be careful not to lower the lights so much that we can't see over here. Okay?"

"Okay, let's see if we can pick it up again from measure 17. Okay?"

The rehearsal of the first act continued, with nearly an hour of starts and stops, during which Joellen interspersed her comments with numerous "okays." Just before the break, she announced, "Let's take about a fifteen-minute break. Okay?" Suddenly, from behind the stage, she heard a male voice loudly shout "okay" in a derogatory, mocking tone of voice. Both she and Jeff demanded to know who had spoken, but no one would own up to it once they realized the directors were upset. After a few tense moments, during which the positive mood had been shattered, Joellen allowed the break to begin.

After the rehearsal, Jeff and Joellen reflected on the rehearsal and planned for the next. Joellen, still smarting from the remark made before the break, said, "I'd sure like to know who the smart-aleck is behind that stage. I'm not going to put up with that anymore. Okay? What can you do to help me? I feel trapped down there in the orchestra pit."

Jeff knew immediately that he would either brush the comment aside or face the truth. He decided on the latter. "Joellen, I don't think you ever realize how many times you say the word 'okay' when you stop to give directions. You use it with almost everything you say. It becomes overbearing. It is a habit, and I don't think you are aware of it. I assume the comment came from a boy enrolled in Mrs. Daniels' speech class where they are learning to listen for and avoid unnecessary language habits."

"Really?"

"Yes, Joellen. Saying 'okay' or 'you know' or 'uh' without meaning becomes a distraction. After awhile, it gets in the way of what you really mean to say. I have to admit, even though students should never be disrespectful, that I can understand how tempting it might have been to make that remark tonight."

Embarrassed, Joellen said she'd immediately work to improve. She thanked Jeff for his honesty. She began focusing less on her feelings of retribution and more on what she could do to change.

Some Other Unnecessary Sayings

1. "like, like, like" (this really dates you as a beginner)
2. "you know what I mean"? (No, I really don't, and you say it so often, I don't think you do either.)
3. "oh, my—oh my, those kids will never get this." (Retire now or go work somewhere else!)

Be a good role model for students in the way you speak. Use correct grammar. Listen to yourself. Tape record a rehearsal and do a self-critique. Listen and critique interviews of athletes on television and empathize with those whose language skills make them appear to be ignorant. You don't want people to think that you can't put your thoughts together effectively. Avoid bad habits. Make eye contact with those with whom you are speaking. Expect kids to mimic and poke fun at you if you are anything less than your best.

TIP 35

~

Teach the Standards

There are state and national content standards for most every subject area, including music. Yet not all teachers appear to know what they are. Get a copy. Most can be downloaded from the Internet. Get a copy of the core knowledge content guidelines. Know what you should teach at each grade, and quit teaching the objectives that don't relate to the standards but *you* might enjoy doing.

Most all music standards documents delineate what students should know and be able to do before graduating from high school, such as those from MENC: National Association for Music Education.*

1. Singing, alone and with others, a varied repertoire of music.
2. Performing on instruments, alone and with others, a varied repertoire of music.
3. Improvising melodies, variations, and accompaniments.
4. Composing and arranging music within specified guidelines.
5. Reading and notating music.
6. Listening to, analyzing, and describing music.
7. Evaluating music and music performances.
8. Understanding relationships between music, the other arts, and disciplines outside the arts.
9. Understanding music in relation to history and culture.

---

*Source: Consortium of *National Arts Education Associations, National Standards for Arts Education: What Every Young American Should Know and Be Able to Do in the Arts* (Reston: VA: MENC, 1999).

Most states and many districts have compiled model lessons aligned with each standard. Find samples, modify them to fit your unique needs, and utilize them. Only when all teachers get on the same bus going the right direction will all children have an opportunity to receive a comprehensive, high-quality education in each content area.

TIP 36

~

Utilize Technology

The younger generation typically has a leg up on their elders when knowing how to use technology. Those in high school and college have grown up with computers, VCRs and DVDs, video games, the Internet, iPods, Palm Pilots, and numerous other technical gadgets. They adapt quickly and instinctively seem to know how to operate the newest devices and navigate the latest communication systems.

But when it comes to the classroom, technological advancements tend to lag behind. Music teachers deserve access to a computer as high-powered as any in the school. They need synthesizers, electronic pianos and keyboards, PCs, laptops, LCD projectors, video libraries, recorders, and the list goes on and on.

No longer can a general music classroom be equipped with just a piano and student chairs. Students deserve so much more. Demand nothing less than the best.

Utilize technology. Work smarter rather than harder. Allow the techno-generation to show you what they know. Then utilize it and find yourself regenerated and excited about all teaching music can offer.

TIP 37

~

Assess Student Progress

Should students' grades in music classes be based on their attendance and behavior or their ability to meet instructional and performance objectives? Unfortunately, the former is often a more prevalent practice. This needs to change. All factors might be considered, but to avoid some form of individual skill and knowledge assessment is ineffective practice.

Even if the grading scale at your school utilizes the S+, S, S–, U scoring system, the teacher should be capable of justifying each individual student's grade. Develop an assessment system that enables you to work with large numbers of students. Assessments do not always have to be in the form of paper and pencil tests. They can be both objective and subjective. Utilize technology that will reduce paperwork and make the task easier.

Students and parents will become more serious and accountable about your classes when they know there will be a fair, individualized, and comprehensive assessment of their progress. And an analysis of your assessments should reflect the effectiveness of your teaching and guide your decisions about instruction.

TIP 38

~

Never Give More Than Three Directions at a Time

Yvonne and Dave team-taught the beginning clarinet classes at Central Elementary School. For the most part, they got along well and were effective teachers. However, Yvonne had begun to notice that fewer students were choosing to play clarinet and that retention rates among clarinet players was the lowest of all the other instruments. Reflecting, she recognized the problem and the reasons why it persisted.

Yvonne realized that all too often when students didn't play their parts satisfactorily, Dave would stop the rehearsal to give directions. Lost in his thoughts, he sometimes ranted on for a minute or two with his analysis of the mistakes. Yvonne found herself unable to concentrate on what he said, and she could observe from the students' body language that they had completely lost their focus. Interest was waning and students were dropping. Yet, Dave seemed oblivious.

In Yvonne's college conducting classes, her professor taught that rehearsals would be most effective if directors would stop, give no more than three directions or corrections, and then move on. She'd experienced this with her own performing groups and now observed the negative results Dave was achieving. But what would she do?

Team-teaching is effective only when colleagues can analyze, discuss, and work to improve each other's instructional delivery. Yvonne knew she had to talk to Dave and help him internalize how he was disrupting the flow of rehearsals and turning off students. How she approached him and his reaction to her comments could influence their future working relationship.

Growing anxious by continued negative observations and the disinterest from students, Yvonne scheduled a time with Dave after school to discuss her observations and plan for improvement.

Yvonne was courageous and lucky. Not every teacher would have the fortitude and self-confidence to confront a colleague with a potentially sensitive critique. She did, Dave graciously accepted her insights, and together they worked to improve. Their results enabled students to enjoy more classroom involvement, and over time, increasingly focused rehearsals resulted in higher levels of performance.

Reflective Questions

1. Are you aware of how many corrections you suggest when you stop your ensemble?
2. Are you prepared to team-teach with a colleague? What special considerations must be preplanned and discussed?
3. What words would you use to address a colleague in a scenario similar to the one described?
4. How do you build a relationship so that you can speak to a colleague about a distracting personal practice or habit?
5. What strategies would you use to restore a relationship with a colleague that has endured conflict?

TIP 39

~

Don't Rehearse the Violins
While the Trombones Wait

Perhaps it is because trombones were not added to orchestral compositions until Beethoven, or maybe because teachers with a string background don't understand brass instruments, but too many conductors show little regard for the trombonists. It's not a good or courteous practice to stop the rehearsal, repeatedly go over a section with the violin section while the trombones wait, or worse, stop after they've counted 99 measures of rests and have an entrance in the next.

If you give them any time, trombonists will start to play. But it is insensitive and inappropriate to scold young musicians for their inattentiveness when the teacher mismanages a rehearsal. Be aware of time and the involvement of each participant. If the violins come to a rehearsal without the technical ability to play a section, chances are they won't master it within 45 minutes. Schedule a sectional. Send them to an alternative rehearsal room with an assistant or approved volunteer and continue rehearsing the rest of the ensemble. Students quickly know when their time is valued and when it is not. Like their peers in other classes, they will stay focused on the task at hand when the teacher is focused and knows how to manage time.

~

Don't Stand in the Same Place

The conductor's podium is symbolic of authority, expertise, power, and creativity as well as many other things. Yet every teacher knows that standing in one location during an instructional period is an ineffectual practice. So how is a music teacher to conduct a rehearsal without being on the podium?

Jose found himself spending inordinate amounts of rehearsal time correcting his percussionists for their inattention, inappropriate behavior, and missed cues. It seemed as though the students were testing him and that disrupting rehearsals had become a game. Their attitude and antics were having a negative effect on the ensemble and becoming a constant irritant. Confiding his frustrations at the staff lunch table, Mrs. Eggleston suggested to Jose that he move within closer proximity, without making any comments, when the group began to act inappropriately. She advised him to keep the rehearsal going as routinely as possible. "This strategy works in my English classes, and I'm sure you can find a way to make it work in the band room."

That afternoon when the trouble began, Jose continued conducting while he stepped away from the podium. His students kept playing, and the percussionists immediately stopped horsing around. Jose said not a word. And he was amazed at some of the sounds he heard from new vantage points. He discovered an airy baritone saxophone missing several pads and two third trombone players who had been passing notes to friends in the French Horn section.

Jose learned that he could keep more students on task and prevent most problems by stepping off the podium. Most of all, his classroom management improved without having to raise his voice. His ensembles played better because he learned to listen from varied positions in the rehearsal room.

Effective music teachers observe their colleagues. They take notes. And they adopt the effective instructional techniques that enable them to improve their work. And sometimes, the best ideas might come from colleagues outside the music department.

Discussion Questions

- What other effective rehearsal techniques can you share?
- What other classroom management techniques have you observed that music teachers should know?
- How could you change the rehearsal set up to create change and achieve results?

TIP 41

~

Continuously Improve Classroom Management

Good teaching is more than knowing and delivering content in a passive setting. The most knowledgeable individuals, unless they can manage students, never reach their potential as effective teachers. Principals don't like teachers who routinely send the students they can't manage to the office for disciplinary intervention. They know those teachers have little power or authority in their classrooms. Teachers simply must learn how to manage students. They are the single most important factor in students' learning and achievement. Poor classroom management leads to chaos.

Music teachers have a leg up on their colleagues because to be effective, they learn how to motivate and manage students in a multi-sensory, active, hands-on learning environment. They learn how to work with small and large groups in traditional classroom environments, rehearsal facilities, performance halls, hallways, closets, gymnasiums, and football fields. And the best realize that their classroom management skills are always evolving and improving as they discover new ways to maximize learning for all students.

Classroom management involves the development of rules, procedures, and interventions that result in order and respect for others. Effective teachers analyze every aspect of their time and responsibilities supervising students: beginning and ending classes, transitions, small ensemble and large group work, lectures, making lines, handling equipment, and dealing with interruptions. They understand the concept of structure. Students are taught how to work and behave and then held accountable once expectations have been made clear. Effective classroom managers rarely utilize consequences for punitive reasons realizing that it most often leads to power struggles with negative outcomes. Instead, they focus on teaching positive expectations and getting better results.

Most importantly, effective classroom managers have good rapport with students. They are friendly, show empathy, and get to know their students. They focus on relationships. They are flexible, congenial, and fun to be with. They leave their personal problems at home and avoid sarcasm, moodiness, inconsistency, and yelling in class. They may be perfectionists, but they take in stride what kids do and make necessary allowances for individual differences. They always maintain eye contact with students, scan the room, and monitor student body language and facial expressions that mirror interest. They develop an intuition that senses problems before they escalate. They accept responsibility for situations for which they should have been in control.

Deborah was a petite, middle-aged elementary general music teacher. Many of her fifth-grade students were taller. At first look, one would assume students would run all over her. But the opposite was true. Deborah routinely met each group of students at her classroom door with a smile, greeted students by name, and taught specific routines for entering and seating. She assigned classroom helpers to assist with attendance, passing out books, setting up equipment, and other routines.

Once her lessons began, she led activities in singing, movement, theory, creating, and performing with instruments while making connections and integrating what students were learning to their previous and current experiences. Her lessons were fun, strategically paced for the developmental levels of each class and individual. Rarely did students choose to break her rules or fail to participate.

But the real measure of Deborah's command of classroom management came outside the music room. As petite as she was, Deborah's colleagues marveled at the attention she could command from large groups of students in the lunchroom, the playground, or other settings where many of them appeared to be ignored.

What were her secrets? She liked kids, and they sensed it. She had a passion for teaching music, and they sensed it. She was consistent, and they came to expect it and take pride in their ability to meet her expectations. She loved learning, and her students did the same.

Good teachers may never send their students to the office, but here are four reasons why you should:

1. A student is sick or there is blood.
2. A student has threatened another student or an adult.

3. A student has repeatedly refused to follow reasonable directions from an adult.

4. A student has engaged in an illicit activity (e.g., drugs, weapons, cheating, lying)

And yes, good teachers do send students to the office for these reasons.

TIP 42

~

Take a Course in Counseling

Music teachers enjoy an advantage of working with the same students over a multi-year period of time. Because of that extended length of time and the intensity of their work and interactions together, students become more familiar with music teachers than most others. And when they are experiencing a personal crisis or need advice, who do they seek out? Their favorite music teacher—the adult they know will listen to them.

Sebastian was a middle school percussionist. John, his band director, had noticed Sebastian had become withdrawn, but when pushed would suddenly become explosive and physically aggressive with others. But he liked the boy. Following one scuffle with another student over who would play a timpani solo, John knew it was time to intervene.

But what he learned surprised him. Sebastian broke down and cried. Through the sobbing and tears, he shared that his mother was near death suffering from a fast-growing, terminal case of breast cancer. John did his best to console, and Sebastian seemed to listen and perceive an empathetic ear when John shared that his mother, too, was battling cancer.

Music teachers encounter scenarios like this all this time. But without proper training or experience, the responsibility can be daunting. Work with your principal, colleagues, and seek the support of trained professionals when students confide personal information and ask for your help.

Know the laws in your community and state regarding the procedures and expectations for reporting of suspected child abuse. Make sure students understand that there may be times when what they tell you in confidence must be reported to proper authorities or your superiors. Obviously, teachers walk a tightrope when trying to develop, protect, and maintain trust with students. Keep their best interests in mind, use common sense, and you will rarely go wrong.

A course in counseling would be appropriate in every music teacher's resume.

What Do You Think?

Do you think this advice is controversial? Perhaps you don't feel it is appropriate to counsel your students.

The line where inappropriate actions begin is often hard to define. No one expects you to act outside your realm of responsibility. However, teachers must strive to develop positive relationships with their students. To do so, you must listen. You must also suggest appropriate and ethical responses to their actions. Call it counseling or not, your work as a music teacher must be focused on helping students make good choices.

TIP 43

~

Encourage Private Lessons

Among the most unforgettable experiences of accomplished musicians are their private lessons. For most, the memories are filled with fondness for a beloved teacher while a few are best described as a love-hate relationship. Regardless, very few musicians attain an outstanding performance level without the tutelage of a private teacher. There is no more effective teaching arrangement than the apprenticeship or one-on-one instructional approach common with most private music lessons.

Identify potential private teachers in your area. Learn about their experience, teaching style, interest in kids, and their success rate. Talk with parents and people in the community. The word spreads about who is competent, patient, caring, and consistently achieves results. Ask each potential teacher if they will allow their name to be included among a list you will share with parents and students.

Establish a series of meetings with parents. Build the case for seeking a private teacher for each student. Unless parents are informed and understand the benefits of private lessons, many will find other ways to spend their time and money. When they learn that lessons are an expectation, strongly encouraged, and supported by you, most will conform. Make arrangements to assist those students for whom it is clear the cost of private lessons is prohibitive. Performing groups will achieve higher performance standards in correlation to the percentage of students taking private lessons.

Not all students will become virtuosic performers. But all students can benefit from 30 to 60 minutes each week of one-on-one attention, encouragement, guidance, role-modeling, and mentoring. Effective private teachers know they must establish personal rapport and build self-esteem as much as teach music. The influence of a competent, caring teacher lasts a lifetime, no matter the endeavors or fields of study one chooses. Encourage parents whose children are just beginning music study to talk with your veterans. Effective parents learn that an investment in private lessons keeps paying dividends for many years in ways they never imagined.

What Should You Do?

- If the students you teach are poor and cannot afford the cost of lessons?
- To develop a schedule for private lessons during school? Afterschool?
- If a student asks you to be their private teacher? Are there ethical considerations?

TIP 44

~

Record Private Lessons

In our litigious society, if a student makes an accusation or alludes to any kind of inappropriate conduct when working with a teacher, especially in a one-on-one setting, it must be investigated. The ramifications of an idle comment or gesture can become damaging. Often, it is the teacher that appears to be "guilty until proven innocent." A reputation which takes years to build can be ruined within a second.

Other students in a classroom can be corroborators when a student accuses an adult or a peer of inappropriate behavior. It is also helpful when other adults observe an encounter. But music teachers, by the nature of their discipline, find themselves vulnerable while teaching private lessons. It makes no difference your gender, age, experience, or reputation. One accusation is enough to blemish a stellar reputation.

Don't be foolish. Require parents to observe private lessons for a prescribed period of time. Structure the time and help put both student and parents at ease. Encourage them to observe your interactions with their child and the type of rapport you establish. In written form, share your expectations and the process for which you will mutually communicate progress, good work, or problems. Document anything that takes place or is shared by a student during a lesson that "sets off red flags."

Video or audiotape lessons. Explain how you will utilize recordings of each lesson to help the student learn and grow. It is good practice to listen, reflect, and demonstrate how to play. But too many teachers fail to utilize recordings. Share them with parents. Keep back-up copies in case they would ever be needed.

Maintain clear and open visibility through the door and windows to your studio. Discuss standard practices and policies with your colleagues. You may feel more comfortable with the door always slightly open. The days of one-on-one private instruction behind closed doors may be over.

Summary:
Another Perspective on Instruction and Professional Performance
Superstars, Backbones, and Mediocres

From your college statistic classes, you'll recognize the shape in the figure below as the bell curve. In any population (or class of students), what falls within one standard deviation above or below from the center line represents approximately two-thirds of the sample group. Those are the "regular" students in your classes. The remaining one-third—one-sixth at either end of the curve—represent those students with special learning needs (usually with individualized education programs in special education) or the brightest on the other end—students identified as gifted and talented.

When teachers are asked which group demands most of their attention and energy, a majority of teachers identify the special needs group.

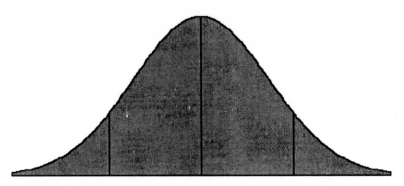

Figure III.1

Imagine your musical ensembles. Do the math. Likely, you discover a similar percentage of students in each category.

When principals contemplate the bell curve and consider their staffs, they envision those professionals who are the backbones of their schools. And they also know those whose performance is described as mediocre. And every staff has its superstars. Deep inside, you know who belongs in each category. Like teachers, principals indicate that the mediocres dominate most of their time and cause them the most worries.

Try this strategy. Give the mediocres their fair amount of attention, but focus your utmost attention and energies in fulfilling the needs of your superstars. Teaching will become more fun and rewarding.

The backbones will lean toward whichever end group gets the most attention of the leader. Focus on the superstars, and the bell curve will skew to the right.

Reflective Questions

1. Within your staff, where would you place yourself: mediocre, backbone, or superstar?
2. Within your staff, where would your principal place you: mediocre, backbone, or superstar?

Self-Assessment Guide, Part III:
Establishing Effective Practices That Support Instruction

How to Use This Assessment Guide

Reflecting privately, or with the support of others, assess your current professional performance, or your preparation for the profession, along the continuum of responses provided in the chart (the numbered items correspond with the tips in the preceding section). There are no right answers; just be honest with yourself. When you are finished, your assessment might reveal needs and areas for further skill development.

You might also encourage a teacher, a friend, or a mentor to share with you how each perceives your professional work and compare and reflect together.

Informal self-assessment and evaluation are important endeavors for all professionals. If you frequently engage in reflective activities you should be well prepared for any outcomes of formal evaluation processes.

My preparation and/or professional performance skills indicate that I . . .	Strongly Disagree	Disagree	Neutral	Agree	Strongly Agree	No Opinion, No Response
18. approach the profession with a sound educational philosophy.						
19. work with a clear sense of direction.						
20. possess the skills to be a star performer in the classroom.						
21. demonstrate punctuality and organization, and use instructional time wisely.						
22. capitalize on the first moments of every class and provide a motivational set.						
23. use time wisely and stay within prescribed times for lessons and classes.						
24. plan ahead and deal effectively with unexpected interruptions.						
25. teach technical skills at a speed that students can learn.						

My preparation and/or professional performance skills indicate that I . . .	Strongly Disagree	Disagree	Neutral	Agree	Strongly Agree	No Opinion, No Response
26. understand how to achieve respect from students and adults.						
27. motivate students to want to learn.						
28. focus more on personal accountability and growth rather than competition against others.						
29. avoid stereotyping.						
30. participate in the development of my own daily schedule.						
31. easily learn and remember names.						
32. treat people fairly.						
33. structure my classes to disallow bullying.						
34. use correct grammar and avoid colloquial language.						
35. teach to the national music standards.						
36. use technology to enhance lessons and work smarter.						
37. effectively assess and report student progress.						
38. give clear directions.						
39. manage effective rehearsals and engage all learners.						
40. move about the classroom.						
41. continuously improve classroom management skills.						
42. show sensitivity to students' human needs.						

My preparation and/or professional performance skills indicate that I . . .	Strongly Disagree	Disagree	Neutral	Agree	Strongly Agree	No Opinion, No Response
43. encourage students to take private lessons.						
44. never work with a student alone in a setting that could lead to reproach.						

~

PART IV

TIPS THAT ENHANCE THE PROFESSION

Art is not the "icing on the cake," but the "yeast in the bread."

—Author Unknown

A school system without parents at its foundation is just like a bucket with a hole in it.

—Rev. Jesse Jackson

TIP 45

~

Be an Advocate for the Arts

Music teachers must become active in arts advocacy, not just for the sake of music, but for all the arts. To develop effective efforts requires strategic planning. There are numerous state and national research and advocacy groups. They encourage and welcome involvement.

Ideally, there would be an active grass-roots arts advocacy program in each school community. Don't expect others to do the work for you. Convene a meeting of your arts colleagues in your district (you may be surprised how infrequently, if at all, they meet). Gather current and accurate information (available on the Web), develop a plan, promote and stay with it. Inform and teach your community about the value of arts in people's lives. Advocacy is not a one-shot initiative.

In your plan, it is recommended that you include:

- strategies to actively engage and involve the community in your instructional program, both inside and outside the schools. Identify key community leaders that will join and actively support your political advocacy efforts
- regular reports and information to the board of education. Seek continuous support and policies that promote a healthy arts environment in schools
- support from the superintendent and principals to garner a clear articulation of the value of arts education and programming for all students

- a listing of program offerings in all schools in all arts areas at all grade levels
- an aggressive professional development plan for arts educators that demonstrates commitment to quality instruction, continuous improvement, and arts experiences for all students
- connections and involvement with state and national arts research and advocacy organizations
- a persistent public relations program that raises awareness and value of the arts based on research, pertinent community data, and current information. Build connections within the community with active artists and arts lovers who can provide visibility and credibility to arts activities. Include business, government, higher education, and service organization leaders
- the development of a personal statement for each arts educator and collect testimonials from students and parents. Shine and don't whine! Be ready to make your personal arts advocacy statement in a clear and concise manner at any moment.

There is no better way to advocate the arts than by getting people involved in firsthand experiences. Communities that value and show support for arts programs now will give their children an advantage in the future workforce. Learners must be equipped with more than cognitive and technical skills. Brighter opportunities will be enjoyed by students who can get along with others, solve problems, show self-discipline, display concern and empathy, think creatively, and communicate ideas in expressive ways. The arts provide *all* students the chance to learn those critical skills and much more!

TIP 46

~

Understand the Child of Poverty

Ozzie and Harriet don't live in most communities anymore. Instead of the two-parent, stay-at-home-mom stereotype from the 1950s, a majority of children today grow up in a single-parent or blended-family home, and increasingly more of them are poor.

High school music performance groups have traditionally catered to students from affluent families. Their parents have the means to purchase expensive instruments, provide private lessons, and afford all the hidden costs that become associated with extracurricular involvement. As a result, music programs have a reputation of being exclusive rather than inclusive, and in changing communities where the level of affluence is diminishing, fewer numbers of students can afford to continue their involvement in music groups. Participation rates spiral downward to the dismay of teachers.

So effective teachers learn how to change, recruit, and include the students from poverty. They find instruments for those who cannot afford one, sponsors for those who cannot pay participation fees or afford uniforms, and arrange transportation to practices and performances for students who would otherwise be left behind. They shed their biases and attitudes toward students and families without means, gain better understanding of poverty, build relationships and understandings, and extend invitations to all. They help break down barriers. Poverty is relative to one's experiences. Not everyone grows up in generational poverty—some cases are situational. Effective music teachers learn the hidden rules of poverty and help children learn to be successful in the middle class setting of schools.

Most of all, they care and strive to provide every child with a quality music education. The most deliberate celebrate numerous success stories. And they help countless students become involved in their schools, appreciate the arts, find their niche, and pull themselves up from unfortunate situations.

Recommended Readings

To gain insights into how people living in poverty, the middle class, or wealth interact with each other and the rules and expectations that typically govern schools, read Dr. Ruby Payne's *A Framework for Understanding Poverty* (2005) and *Bridges out of Poverty: Strategies for Professionals and Communities* (2006).

~

Promote the "Mozart Effect"

The hypothesis that the study of music, especially exposure to the music of Mozart, can make one smarter has received considerable, sometimes overstated attention from the popular media. Experiments by researchers such as Frances Rauscher and Gordon Shaw have shown a temporary improvement in ability to discern certain spatial relationships with exposure to Mozart's music. All musicians understand the benefits of the disciplined study of music on spatial and temporal tasks. Yet, there remain those in the public who need to be convinced.

In today's culture, when parents notice that their child is active and distractible, they consult with a physician and often seek medication as part of an intervention plan to help the child achieve success. Parents would overwhelm doctors with requests if they thought a pill could make their children smarter. Yet, perhaps it's not a pill that will meet that need after all, but rather a recording of a Mozart piano sonata that could positively influence learning and memory.

Former Georgia governor Zell Miller found the research findings to be convincing enough that he implemented a jump-start learning program that provided tapes or CDs of Mozart's music to all parents of newborns in his state. Given time, the effects will be evident in Georgia classrooms. Research also shows that exercise increases the flow of oxygen to the brain and that a healthy diet and vitamin supplements increase brain power. Good music can reduce stress. There is no doubt that exposure to good music increases the development of the neural pathways that enable the brain to function at higher levels. And it stimulates healing and creativity.

For ages, mothers have known what is best. They've insisted on getting enough sleep, eating right, and playing. They've also sung to their babies. Music teachers have an obligation to teach today's parents to add some Mozart to their child's prescription for a good life.

TIP 48

~

Learn the Value of Public Relations

Kenneth's high school orchestra program was well regarded throughout Central City. Members of the city school board routinely recognized Kenneth and the orchestra program for high levels of achievement. Throughout the community, ordinary citizens associated the high school orchestra with top quality. This perception existed despite the fact that many people had never spent much time listening to it. How did this happen? People were fed a steady stream of information about the orchestra and its achievements through the local newspaper.

Kenneth was a public relations expert as well as an effective teacher. His groups became untouchable during tough economic times. They became a symbol of pride for the community and represented everything that is good about secondary education. But this didn't happen without a steady, determined public relations program.

Newspaper reporters always received invitations and complimentary tickets to concerts. Their good work was publicly acknowledged. They were also given fact sheets that helped when they wrote follow-up reports. Press releases were routinely issued informing the public of upcoming concerts and cultural events. And Kenneth didn't limit his public relations campaign to the newspaper. He also developed positive relationships with representatives at the local radio stations, the public access television station, and served as webmaster of the orchestra Web site. He was a sought-after speaker.

Public relations tasks and activities must be included in your weekly planning. It must be a responsibility of every music teacher. Good news can be created and controlled. And like bad news, it spreads. Which would you rather have had responsibility for starting?

TIP 49

~

Invite the Mayor to Conduct

Too often music teachers fall prey to the pressures of their daily schedule and the multitude of responsibilities that accompany it. They focus on writing lesson plans, conducting rehearsals, and planning myriad activities focused on meeting students' needs. In the routine of preparing concert after concert, many look at the calendar and realize the limited amount of rehearsal time between events. Their time management skills become instinctive, and every minute with an ensemble becomes precious. Music teachers are very busy people.

But don't be like a horse with blinders. Take time to think how some simple gestures could enhance interest in a future concert. Invite the mayor to conduct. Or identify other key members of the community and draw them in: lawmakers, school board members, the superintendent, a principal, former music teachers, ministers, vendors, or music club members. And if appropriate, don't forget to include your predecessor on that list.

Some music teachers don't realize the influence and support they can achieve by increasing the involvement of their communities in performances. Advertise concerts. Distribute complimentary tickets at senior citizen centers. Empower students to go into the community and perform in nursing homes or at community service clubs, civic events, and parades. And don't forget to schedule high school groups at elementary parent meetings. Give the members of the beginning band, choir, or orchestra program a special invitation to a high school event. It will become a memorable event when younger musicians are invited to play side-by-side with the "big kids."

Music has the power to draw people together and create goodwill within a community. Music teachers must be their own promoters. The most effective are public relations experts. It takes just a few phone calls to involve key people, engage the community, and lay the groundwork for recognition and support of the music program and for yourself.

Befriend and Respect the Custodians

Principals know that custodians (as well as most other classified employees in key support positions) can make or break them. The same applies to music teachers.

Music classrooms are busy places with numerous students that collectively create wear and tear and dust and dirt. Custodians can clean a room, or they can *really* clean it. And an organized, structured, clutter-free music room sends a message to students and others who visit. Experience shows that music teachers who get the best treatment and service have a close, professional, and respectful relationship with the custodial staff.

It doesn't take long in your teaching career for a crisis of some type to occur. That might be realized just before that start of a concert when suddenly a microphone system won't work, special lighting fails, or additional seating is needed. Good custodians always come to the rescue—those who don't care for the music teacher are always out of sight.

Caring custodians have been known to enable students to "somehow" retrieve their forgotten instrument after school hours saving the band director a trip to open the school. Others have volunteered to fix broken instruments and equipment, set up and tear down for special events, and go the extra mile and serve as supporters and boosters behind the scenes in many unique ways.

Publicly acknowledge your custodians. List their names in programs. Include them in special events and celebrations. Teach your students to treat them with respect. Model what you expect from others. Show appreciation and genuinely thank the custodian who makes sure you are safely to your car late at night.

TIP 51

~

Be Active in Your Community

Get to know people in your community. Play or sing for Kiwanis and Rotary meetings. Join service groups when asked and your time permits. Roll up your sleeves and work side by side as volunteers strive to raise funds for their community projects. Likely, when you've earned their respect, your friends will support the music program when you need it.

Educators differ on opinions about whether they should live in the same community in which they work. District demographics are varied. Some will discover housing to be too expensive while others will find nothing to be desirable or comfortable. Some teachers don't want their students to know where they live. Most districts have relaxed or done away with residency requirements for teachers.

Regardless of your housing preference, it is highly recommended that music teachers adopt a high profile in their school communities. Never underestimate the influence and leadership role that comes with working with young students, especially high schoolers. Citizens will revere those music teachers whose commitment to and care of children is obvious. Watch the movies *Mr. Holland's Opus* or *Music of the Heart* if you want to see touching examples.

Perform in churches. Have a continual supply of students coached and ready with solo and ensemble selections to fulfill requests for meetings and civic functions. Showcase your students and your music program at all times.

Believe it or not, in many communities, high school band and choir directors wield influence on a level with that of their principal—or more! Accept that responsibility. Be a professional. Pay your dues. Enjoy the limelight.

TIP 52

~

Write Grants

There never seems to be enough money in school budgets to adequately and equitably fund all educational initiatives. Music programs can be costly to operate and maintain. The news reports of reductions and elimination of arts and music offerings in schools are all too common. But even where budget deficits don't exist, having enough money to create a first-class music program can be a challenge.

So learn how to write grants. Identify your needs and collect supportive data. Talk with those who have had successful experiences and ask to read copies of their submissions. Enroll in a class or workshop on grant writing. Utilize the Internet to research grant opportunities. Sign up on Listservs that can alert you about grant opportunities. Review the grants available through state and federal departments of education, state and local arts associations, foundations, businesses, civic and community service groups, and professional associations.

When possible, write grant narratives using a word processor. Once one grant is written, many others could follow a similar format. Don't get discouraged. Your students don't necessarily play all the right notes in their first performances, and you may need several tries to receive a grant.

Remember, you'll never receive anything if you don't try. Don't be jealous of those who do.

TIP 53

~

Never Underestimate a Booster Club

Robert was a 20-year veteran high school band director. He began his career in the Mayfield School District and had enjoyed a successful tenure until the school district's tax base collapsed after the city's largest employer and manufacturing company relocated. Within a year, enrollment in the school's 150-piece marching band dropped by 30 members as families moved from the district, and many more were fearful that they would be forced to leave. The local economy was thrust into a downward spiral. When voters rejected several tax increases, the schools were forced to drastically reduce expenditures. Robert's music programs, along with other extracurricular activities, were slated for devastating cuts.

Robert's reputation as a successful band director was well known throughout the state. As such, it became front page news when the school board's decision was announced to cut the band program. Complicating his situation was an offer from school administrators in a rival district to interview for an open position. Robert was a loyal Mayfield employee. But realizing he couldn't control what was happening in his district, he considered his options and quietly began talking with officials in the other locale.

But word leaked out about his possible move. Once Robert's music boosters learned that he was being aggressively courted elsewhere and fearful that they would lose him, they began a grass-roots campaign to save their music programs—and Robert's job. What developed over subsequent months, like never before in Mayfield, was a parent-organized and supported school referendum that resulted in an historic 60 percent approval rating at the polls.

No one believed it could happen, but it did. School officials clearly under-estimated the power of the booster group. They also failed to recognize the influence Robert leveraged with his boosters.

In contrast, Rochelle's relationship with her booster group could best be described as tenuous. Rochelle was distant. She didn't always participate in booster activities or attend their meetings. She'd experienced several tense conflict situations with students and parents, some who were influential members of the booster club. At times, her interactions with people were described as unethical. She was not well liked by students. It was evident that the quality of her performing groups diminished each year.

Rochelle's rocky relationship turned for the worse when booster members began voicing their complaints to her principal, the district superintendent, and members of the board of education. They began increasing pressure—unrelenting at times. It became apparent that Rochelle was incapable of reversing the perceptions of others, and she was counseled to either vacate her position as band director or face termination from the district.

Music teachers, parent boosters, and school administrators can relate to these scenarios. They are repeatedly played out across the nation. The lesson to be learned is that music booster groups, when given the motivation, either positive or negative, can become one of the most powerfully mobilized politi-cal interest groups in the community. Effective music teachers know that to build strong relationships with their booster groups, they must:

- work for quality at all times
- earn the respect, not only of students, but also their parents
- treat booster groups professionally and with respect
- attend all booster functions and play an active role in meetings
- facilitate the boosters' interest in school governance
- fully understand the influence of the teacher, but never abuse it
- provide leadership and guidance that enable the boosters to achieve goals that benefit the music program and school.

There never seems to be enough money in any school budget to fully support a vital music program. Music boosters are essential. Recognize the importance of building relationships with people. Treat them with respect. And be willing to provide leadership when it is appropriate and in the best interest of the music program and students.

TIP 54

~

Create a Program for Performances

Some may think it is too much work, but it is important to create a written program for each performance. It serves as documentation of your work and becomes a part of your school's written history similar to an annual yearbook. Even at the elementary level, a written program is essential.

Besides the order of performed works, list the names of the student performers. Proofread to insure that all names are included and spelled correctly. Additionally, include the names of the students' classrooms, music department staff, the school administration, the board of education, and other individuals who helped prepare the program or deserve a word of thanks. Learn how to utilize a word processor and a desktop publishing program so that you can produce top-quality work.

A written program enables you the opportunity to creatively explain objectives, state goals, clarify expectations, and inform guests of upcoming events. It can serve a key role with the development of public relations. If your ambitions are high and the program becomes expensive, seek advertisers who will offset some of the costs. Expect to find copies displayed proudly in homes of your students. They often become valued memorabilia displayed at graduation parties and other significant events in the community life.

Do a quality job. Fifty years from now, when historians and music lovers are reflecting on the past, you hope they will be impressed by your work and pick up an idea or two for their programs.

Remember

Proofread, proofread, proofread.

And always make sure your principal approves a copy of the program in advance and receives a final copy for his files afterward.

Furthermore

Make audio and video recordings of your programs. Create an archived historical music library and share copies with your school library as well. You are creating history and devote the necessary time and resources to recording it well.

TIP 55

~

Train Volunteers and Chaperones

Volunteers can be vital to the success of any program. They can contribute manpower and services that could never be accomplished exclusively with paid personnel. In music programs, volunteers may also have special designations as chaperones, boosters, concession stand workers, contest organizers, sectional assistants, nurses, cooks, equipment managers, drivers, "go-fors," or student helpers. Treat them well. They can make or break you.

Spend time training your volunteers. Create a handbook that lists expectations and descriptions of the responsibilities, duties, and work that they are asked to fulfill. Check with them often. Show appreciation. Work beside them and get to know them. Listen as they share their perceptions of your work and the music program. Collect their testimonials of the benefits they gain from working with your program.

Many school districts require background checks or other information about volunteers before they can work with children. This is good practice for your program as well as the volunteer and the reasons need to be shared before entering into a relationship, no matter how well you know the individual. It is never a good idea to place a volunteer in a one-on-one isolated setting with a student. An acceptable ratio among students and volunteer chaperones in most situations is one for every 8 to 10 students.

Keep information about volunteers in individual files. What you gather can be used for a variety of purposes such creating special features about them in your newsletters, learning about their birthdays, occupations, and special interests.

Treat volunteers with courtesy and respect. Publicly acknowledge their contributions. And realize that volunteers can become a force of their own that can quickly veer out of control if left to themselves. Maintain a proper hierarchy of authority between paid and volunteer personnel. Allow opportunities for everyone involved with your program, paid and volunteer, to evaluate the relationship and suggest ideas for continuous improvement.

TIP 56

~

Sing, Dance, Create, and Perform

The principal of Center Street Elementary School visited the kindergarten classroom at the beginning of the school year and asked the students, "How many of you can sing?" Typically, most every child enthusiastically raised a hand. Then he asked, "How many of you can dance?" and received a similar response. Sometimes, a student would stand to demonstrate. "How many of you think you could jump 10 feet in the air?" he challenged. In their minds, the students imagined themselves in midair leaping like professional basketball players.

Then he went to the sixth grade classroom and asked the same questions. "How many of you can sing?" A few hands sheepishly were raised. "How many of you can dance?" Stealing anxious glances around the room, a few girls raised their hands. None of the students thought they could jump very high. "How many of you can write or compose music"? No responses. "Do you like to perform?" Some heads nodded favorably, but it was clear that peer pressure was taking a negative toll. Fear of publicly acknowledging what others might view as "nerdy" kept many heads bowed.

Later at a staff meeting, he shared the results from his informal poll. As he reported the findings, he asked, "Why is it that our students lose their confidence and ability to think they are invincible as they progress through our school? Do we pound it out of them? Why do they have to acquire their inhibitions and think 'I can't' instead of 'I can'?"

Try this informal test for yourself. The responses will typically be the same. More importantly, work with your colleagues to reverse the trend.

Equip your students with confidence to maintain their interest and enthusiasm for the performing arts. Create a school climate where students can be expressive, move, and use their imaginations without feeling someone will poke fun. They'll participate, learn, and enjoy themselves when they feel comfortable and are taught that it's acceptable and "cool" to sing and dance in front of their peers.

~

Teach Audience Etiquette

Jocelyn liked to muse with her husband, Zach, as they would drive together to one of her elementary music programs, saying, "I'll bet this will be a 30-cap night!" It irritated her that so many people attending her programs, especially the men, didn't know enough to remove their hats. People got up and walked around, and parents allowed their kids to run rampant. It seemed to her that there was a correlation between the number of ball caps and how restless and talkative each audience would later become. She taught in a school with moderately high levels of poverty and assumed that unfamiliarity with middle class customs might be the source of the problem. But she'd also noticed increased incidents of noisy crowds at concerts in more affluent schools. She and her husband had become concerned that no one, particularly the principal, seemed to do anything to help control the audiences.

Determined to see conditions change, Jocelyn asked that this issue be discussed at the next music department meeting. She was relieved to hear several of her colleagues share the same concerns, but disappointed that some of the old guard thought nothing could ever be done and were unwilling to try.

So Jocelyn said, "If we are supposed to teach performance skills to the kids, maybe we also need to teach audience etiquette as well. Maybe people act the way they do because they just don't know any better." Then Jim, the senior-most middle school choir director, countered, saying, "But I'm surely not going to stand up there and tell the parents how to behave. They'll be insulted and complain to the principal."

"But maybe that's what it will take to get her attention," said Jocelyn. "We have a problem. It's getting worse in my school and probably in each of yours as well. I think we have a responsibility to establish the expectations we want from our students as well as our audience. Is it too much to expect them to sit and listen while a song is being performed?

"No," said Rachel, a general music teacher from Riverside Elementary School. "We just have to find a nice way to make our points and consistently convey the message."

The teachers further deliberated and planned, then agreed to print the rules of audience etiquette in all of their forthcoming programs, to orally address the reasons, and to request cooperation in the most professional manner. What follows is their consolidated list for programs.

Audience Etiquette for Riverside City Schools Music Programs

- Wait to be seated between selections or between acts. It is distracting to the audience and performers when someone enters during the performance
- Avoid trips to the restroom or drinking fountain while the program is in progress. Please wait until intermission
- Please do not wear hats inside the performance area
- Please do not bring food or drinks into the performance hall
- Please do not talk, whisper loudly, crack chewing gum, or make noises during the performance. This is very distracting to the performers and to others in the audience
- Please turn off all cell phones, pagers, and other electronic devices that may distract the performance. These items may also interfere with our sound system
- Do not allow small children to play with keys, coins, or toys that make noise. Keep children seated with you and out of the aisles. If your children become upset, start crying, or create a distraction for others, please remove them from the performance hall until they are ready to return
- Please applaud at the end of each selection, unless it is a multi-movement work for which applause is appropriate at the very end
- Please do not shout out names of students and make inappropriate comments. Students are being assessed on their ability to display performance skills. They have been taught not to wave at members of the audience. Please help them avoid that temptation by refraining from inappropriate behavior while in the audience

- Please do not take pictures that require the use of a flash or use recording equipment that will become distracting to the performers and others in the audience
- Enjoy the program. We appreciate your cooperation and our collective efforts to provide the highest level performance standards for all students and listeners.

After just a few months, Jocelyn began to see positive results. Most people were very cooperative. Several parents commented that they were very happy to see expectations for the audience addressed—and in a positive way. Her principal commended her for her efforts. Jocelyn and her colleagues became comfortable speaking to audiences before each program began, setting the expectations, and reinforcing them when necessary.

Jocelyn's approach reinforced a valuable lesson. She realized it was wrong to become frustrated and angry with the performance of her students unless she had clearly taught them and made sure they learned the lessons. She had to ascertain they could achieve independence and perform capably when expected.

She also realized, if she wanted better results, that it was necessary to teach the adults as well as the children.

The Bottom Line

A huge part of a principal's job is to listen to people describe problems. You will be certain to gain attention and respect if your practice is to briefly identify the problem but also offer a solution for consideration.

TIP 58

~

Pay Your Accompanists

Blessed are piano accompanists. They can make or break a performance. They know their parts—and yours. The best have covered numerous mistakes for soloists or large ensembles and made them sound good. They know how to follow, anticipate changes, and go with the flow. They are talented individuals. Make sure that you provide them the gratuities they deserve.

Provide your accompanists with:

- original copies of all the music you expect them to play with adequate time to learn it
- a schedule of all rehearsals during which you need their support
- adequate communication and rehearsal time with you prior to meeting with the larger ensemble
- an outline of expectations, reporting times, and concert dress
- invitations to receptions and post-performance activities
- written recognition in programs as well as oral and visible acknowledgment during performances.

Most importantly, compensate your accompanists. Besides pianists, accompanists may include a small ensemble of instrumentalists or numerous other configurations of musicians necessary for selected works. Accomplished accompanists are more than volunteers and should be treated professionally. Determine a standard rate of compensation within your district. Budget adequate amounts. Expect to pay accordingly for the quality your desire.

TIP 59

~

Understand the Needs of the Middle School Adolescent

Blessed are the professionals who *choose* to work with students in the middle grades. They deserve a special place in "teacher heaven." Because of the developmental changes that young adolescents experience during these grades, their emotional, social, and instructional needs are very different from children in elementary or high school. It is not always a positive experience when secondary vocal or instrumental teachers choose to leave the hustle and bustle of high school responsibilities and relocate to the middle school where there is supposedly "less stress and responsibility" without adequate training.

Effective music teachers in the middle grades know what best motivates their students. They create conditions and establish structures that allow the students to be successful. They identify those traditional reward and punishment techniques of elementary school that are no longer effective. They know what will arouse their students' curiosity and how to restructure the curriculum to grab their attention and maintain interest. Lecturing is balanced with hands-on activities.

In the music room, peer relationships become more important than ever. Effective music teachers help students feel good about themselves. They recognize that their students want and need work that enables them to demonstrate and improve their sense of themselves as competent and successful human beings. Teachers nurture students in their drive toward mastery. The best recognize the students who are most creative and teach them that it is okay to fail. They help them accept failure as a part of the experience of success by providing clear, immediate, and constructive feedback.

Most of all, effective middle level music teachers nurture students as they develop their personalities. They encourage curiosity, experimentation, and originality. They help students identify the knowledge and skills they possess within their grasp. Effective teachers, by modeling, continually encourage and empower students to process information at higher levels.

TIP 60

~

Get Along with the Coaches

Why is it that so many music teachers and coaches, at all levels of instruction, can't get along? Is it because of turf issues, self-interests and egos, obsessive interest in individual students, or that they are simply predisposed to challenge each other and argue? Why can't the relationship between the music teacher and coach showcased in the classic movie *Mr. Holland's Opus* become the norm? Tension and discord leave students in the cold. There has to be a way work together.

That way starts when music teachers take the lead in building strong interpersonal relationships, not only with coaches, but also with all their colleagues. Yet, too many stay within the confines of the band or choir room, avoiding adult interactions and involvement in activities of the school. When issues arise that force students to choose between music and athletic events, the interpersonal relationships and respect that, if it existed, could help adults compromise, is missing. The student becomes a pawn, and if the athletic event takes priority, the music teacher more often than not becomes negative, uncooperative, and seeks retribution in a variety of ways. Everyone loses. The outcomes lead to further exclusivity of both music and athletics. Over time, each activity will benefit from an attitude of inclusivity.

Get out of the band or choir room. Visit the lounge. Don't become a "lounge lizard" or engage in the gossip that is sometimes rampant there, but realize the importance of time spent building relationships with colleagues throughout the school. When music teachers are viewed by others with respect and they recognize that students' best interests are your focus, many conflicts can be avoided. Don't expect others to come to you. Make the effort and go to them. Talk about sports, weather, news, and local interests. Be a friend. Be a willing participant in resolving conflicts. The time invested will reap many rewards and help many students enjoy participation in activities of their choice. They will also aspire to be like their role models.

TIP 61

~

Engage the Community

Who are your key constituencies and stakeholders within your community? They are those, who when you actively seek their involvement, will develop partnerships and support your program in numerous ways. In return, they will gain fulfillment enriching the musical experiences of your students and extend their appreciation and learning about music.

Seek out these groups and individuals, invite them to become involved, provide incentives that create a win-win relationship, and benefit from their unlimited support:

- business leaders
- civic and service club leaders and members
- government leaders and employees
- college and university administrators and personnel
- senior citizens
- retired teachers (especially retired music teachers)
- freelance musicians
- clergy and church musicians
- piano teachers
- after school personnel
- private music instructors
- artists
- cultural center and museum personnel
- the athletic community

- dance studio owners and personnel
- the YMCA and YWCA
- social service agency personnel
- early childhood, preschool, and Kindermusik instructors.

This list is not intended to be comprehensive in any way. Each community is unique. Work with your colleagues to build strong relationships with the key constituents within yours.

TIP 62

~

Make Ethical Decisions

Randy and Phil were college roommates and best friends. Once they graduated, they were fortunate to fulfill their dream of obtaining similar positions as high school choral directors in school districts less than 30 miles apart. They found an apartment and continued rooming together during their first year as teachers. They enjoyed sharing and discussing experiences from work, learning together, and commiserating when situations were tough.

In November, both were responsible for auditions and assigning leads in preparation for the spring musical. They both decided to program My Fair Lady. Following the initial tryouts, they discovered they were confronting a similar dilemma.

"I'm struggling with a problem, Phil," Randy shared one night during dinner. "I'm struggling with who should get the lead in the musical. I auditioned three capable singers. Bethany is simply a natural—beautiful voice with attractive features and self-confidence. Rosetta is even more talented but doesn't have any experience. I'm concerned that she appears to have little parental support. And the third is the daughter of the principal. She's capable, but of the group, more like a prima donna. I don't know which one is the best choice."

"Randy, you won't believe it, but I'm struggling with almost an identical set of circumstances. Only one of my potential leads is the daughter of the school board president."

Both felt confident that their audition procedures had been fair and impartial. The most capable singers and performers had emerged to play the role of Eliza. In both schools, the final selection rested with the choral director and was a personal and subjective choice. Only one could be chosen with the runner-up to be named as an understudy with another lesser role in the production. The third would be denied a part. Both Phil and Randy expressed concerns about public perceptions should they select the daughter of the principal or the school board president. The musical was a high profile event in both districts.

Randy selected Rosetta despite her limited experience. The understudy role went to Bethany, and he denied the principal's daughter any part. Phil, on the other hand, selected the school board president's daughter for the lead. Admittedly, he knew he was seeking favor and trying to placate an influential member of the school community. The decision rested uncomfortably with him, but over time he thought it would prove to be in his best interest.

Randy figured his tenure and support would come to a quick ending at his school. But he was wrong. His principal never said a word about the selection, continued to provide strong support, and intervened on Phil's behalf when Bethany's parents cried foul.

People within both districts soon realized *My Fair Lady* was being staged by the two friends. They enjoyed observing the young men's progress and comparing the final performances. Randy's production proved to be a disappointment. The school board member's daughter made several mistakes and was unable to project her voice or stay in tune. Phil's Eliza surprised everyone and exceeded expectations. She became an overnight celebrity. A voice teacher from the state university sought her out and offered a full scholarship. The musical was the best the school had ever produced.

Music teachers will often find themselves facing important ethical decisions. Do what is right. Be fair and consistent. Don't allow politics, internal pressures, and perceptions to influence your thinking and decision-making processes. Be true to yourself and others.

Discussion Topic

Have you ever been asked this question in an interview: "Why should I (we) hire you from among the other candidates for this job?"

1. Brainstorm answers.
2. Share them with a colleague
3. Do you think you've discovered an answer that is the appropriate final cadence for an interview?

How about considering this response?—(but only if you are capable of delivering the goods)—"You should hire me because I am the most ethical person you will find. My work ethic and training are second to none. You can trust me. I won't disappoint you. I will not drop the ball. You can depend upon me. The focus of my work and the tough decisions I will be asked to make will always be based on what is best for kids—and for this school."

> Wrong is wrong even if everyone does it. Right is right even if no one does it.
>
> —Author Unknown

~

Organize Productive Fundraisers

It's unlikely you'll find yourself working in a school that can provide a budget sufficient enough to meet the needs of a growing music program. Fundraising will likely be a part of your responsibilities. Learn to do it well. Consult with representatives of reputable fundraising companies. Ask them to meet with you and others from your program that share responsibilities for sales projects and explain the services they can provide. Don't be afraid to ask for references and write a contract for services. At all times, follow policies established by your board of education and administrative procedures.

Recognize the expertise and experience of fundraising professionals. Treat them with respect. Their service can become an invaluable asset to your program's survival in tough economic times. Don't delegate responsibilities to parents without periodically checking on how things are going.

Coordinate your fundraising efforts with others in the school. If possible, avoid a music program sale when the athletic department has one scheduled. Realize that your community is canvassed by multiple groups trying to raise funds. Plan fewer sales that can generate greater profits.

Get organized. Plan for the arrival of the sales representative. Work with them. Nothing could become more damaging for your success or perception within the community than to treat these professionals unfairly. Don't underestimate their influence. They work with dozens of your colleagues. People talk. Give them numerous reasons to say positive things about you.

TIP 64

~

Learn How to Ask Questions

It's not likely that many music teachers had a class in college that devoted very much time to questioning techniques. It is one aspect of teaching that is all too often taken for granted. Yet, it is one of the most important techniques that teachers use to assess their students' understanding. Effective teachers intuitively know how to ask questions, and with training, can get even better.

Part of learning how to ask questions is developing an understanding of how to establish conditions in which students are engaged and receptive. Effective teachers set high expectations and know that students must be challenged to think at higher levels to achieve the deepest levels of understanding. But, first they focus on getting the conditions right.

Effective teachers know how to ask the right questions, at the right time, in the right way, and in the right order and sequence. They incorporate questioning techniques as a part of every instructional process. They understand Bloom's taxonomy and related theories of higher thinking skills. In quick form, you could use this brief outline:

Level 1 (Knowledge): Students will be labeling, identifying, and recalling basic information; teacher prompts questions with "What is . . . ? "Where is . . . ?" "How is . . . ?" "Can you recall . . . ?" "Which one . . . ?"

Level 2 (Comprehension): Students will be defining, discussing, calculating, comparing, inferring, and contrasting; teacher prompts with "How would you contrast . . . ?" "What is the main idea . . . ?" "Can you explain . . . ?" "What can you say about . . . ?"

Level 3 (Application): Students will be selecting, illustrating, organizing, making, and showing; teacher prompts with "How would you use . . . ?" "What examples can you find . . . ?" "How can you show your understanding . . . ?" "What facts would you select to . . . ?"

Level 4 (Analysis): Students will be classifying, comparing, distinguishing, observing, and identifying; teacher prompts with "Why do you think . . . ?" "Can you list the parts . . . ?" "What ideas justify . . . ?" "What evidence can you find . . . ?" "What is the theme . . . ?"

Level 5 (Synthesis): Students will be collecting, creating, formulating, imagining, planning, rearranging, and revising; teacher prompts with "What would happen if . . . ?" "How would you improve . . . ?" "How would you test . . . ?" "How would you change . . . ?"

Level 6 (Evaluation): Students will be appraising, explaining, judging, measuring, testing, and verifying; teacher prompts with "How would you rate . . . ?" "What is your opinion of . . . ?" "How would you justify . . . ?" "How would you prioritize . . . ?" "What would you select . . . ?"

Practice these techniques. Try them with your own children. If you want to know what happened at school, don't ask "What did you do at school today?" Kids most often say, "Nothing!" Instead, ask a question that requires a response higher than the knowledge level. Try something like "Can you list the most important things your teachers said today?" Or perhaps, "What was the theme of your reading lesson?" "How did you know that the weather effects the way instruments might sound?" "How did you figure out that a trombone plays lower as the slide extends?" You'll be surprised by the responses.

Enjoy learning how to ask the right questions in the right way.

TIP 65

~

Show Your Passion and Pride

When you are introduced to strangers and asked what you do, how do you respond? "I'm Barbara Smith, and I'm just the general music teacher at Brown Elementary School." Or do you introduce yourself this way? "I'm Barbara Smith, and I have the best job in the world. I'm privileged to introduce young students at Brown Elementary School to the world of music, inspire their creativity, and to motivate them to think and experience music in the world around them." Maybe that's a bit much, but hopefully you say something more than "I'm just a teacher."

Pride is a motivational force. For most, it is more important than money. And effective music teachers know how to magically instill it in their students. They create performing ensembles that are focused on group pride much more than individual self-interests. They incorporate pride-building skills, tools, and techniques that help their students rise above the mediocre. They teach a strong work ethic—perhaps a more important characteristic for success than a superior talent (see the works of Geoff Colwin, *Talent Is Overrated: What Really Separates World-Class Performers from Everybody Else* [2008], and Malcolm Gladwell, *Outliers* [2008]). Effective music teachers help students set high aspirations and see purpose in their work. They cultivate personal relationships that develop trust and respect. Pride based on the relentless pursuit of a worthwhile cause helps a school improve performance. There is a fundamental correlation between pride and high performing schools.

Always focus on the source of your pride and passion: your students. Education is a noble cause. Remember what you believe in and what is worth fighting for. Let your passion and feelings show. Be a positive example for others.

Students love and respect passionate teachers. They understand what they stand for. They are positive and exciting to be around. They have an aura. They have pride. They focus on learning and avoid negativity. They make things happen when others cave.

TIP 66

~

Create High-Quality
Music with Preschoolers

Increasingly, educators are realizing the critical importance of quality learning experiences for students *before* they enter kindergarten. Research shows that the best time to cultivate a child's language development and physical, emotional, cognitive, and social growth may be before the age of three. Without a doubt, the preschool years are an important time to teach kids to sing, dance, and play. By the time a child reaches age five and enters kindergarten, valuable learning opportunities have been lost.

Teachers who work in early childhood programs know that music is a powerful stimulant that promotes a child's total development. Whether they may have a curriculum to follow or they hit and miss, they know the value of music. It is important that early childhood providers and school music teachers work together to develop quality, sequential musical experiences and learning opportunities for all students.

Whether you prefer the philosophies and methodologies of Orff, Kodaly, Laban, Dalcroze, or other approaches, childhood experts agree that early musical experiences have been important throughout history. Music learning is valued across all cultures and provides children an intrinsic motivation to explore the arts throughout their lives.

And who couldn't enjoy working with preschool children? It is fun!

TIP 67

~

Emphasize the Multiple Intelligences

Most everyone can think of someone with superior cognitive abilities but who also seems to lack social skills and common sense. These individuals often have trouble relating with ordinary humans and completing simple daily tasks. Despite advanced intelligence, their personalities are imbalanced due to weaknesses in physical, emotional, spiritual, or other intelligences. Individuals with lesser abilities but better balance in several areas seem happier and more capable of adjusting to the demands of adult life.

Effective teachers know children who don't seem to fit the mold. They appear to be very smart, yet score poorly on standardized tests. They may be superior students in science, average in social studies, and klutzes in physical education. On the other hand, they may be athletically gifted and able to recall statistics and factual information about sports teams but unable to master math facts. Music teachers have always identified students with superior musical abilities and promoted talent. All students should benefit from an educational program that promotes multiple modes of learning.

For some parents, it is a prized status symbol and critically important that their child be labeled as talented and gifted. But most assessments used to determine that select group of students identify superior functioning abilities only in reading or mathematics. What about the musicians or athletes who excel? Are their gifts not as important?

In the early 1980s, Harvard University professor Howard Gardner helped explain differences in students when he introduced his theory of multiple intelligences. His research showed that individuals possess strengths and preferred learning styles in seven different ways:

1. Linguistic: an advanced ability with meaning and order of words.
2. Logic and mathematics: an advanced ability in mathematical concepts and other complex tasks requiring logical thinking.
3. Musical: an advanced ability to create and understand musical concepts (the one Gardner felt might be first to emerge).
4. Spatial: an advanced ability to think with the mind in pictures and re-create on paper.
5. Body-kinesthetic: an advanced ability to control the movements of the body toward a goal.
6. Interpersonal: an advanced ability to perceive and understand the moods and motivations of others.
7. Intrapersonal: an advanced ability to understand one's own emotions.

Later, Gardner introduced an eighth intelligence, *naturalistic*, an advanced ability to recognize plants, animals, rocks, and other aspects of nature.

Gardner's work and that of many others has influenced the way teachers evaluate students' strengths and structure their lessons. Teachers always knew that young children best learned the sequence of letters by singing the *Alphabet Song* or the names of the states by singing *Fifty Nifty United States*. They always observed students with average academic abilities excel when they could sing or keep rhythm with a pencil. And the closer they began observing, they realized more and more children grasped new concepts with greater enthusiasm when allowed to sing or listen to music.

The rest of the story is recorded in educational journals and a subject of countless professional development workshops for teachers. What music teachers need to understand about these theories is that they have legitimized music instruction in the minds of many of their colleagues. Effective classroom teachers have redesigned their instructional approaches and adopted an interdisciplinary approach that better meets students' diverse needs by teaching to their strengths. Music teachers have the skills that can help their colleagues become even more successful addressing students' musical intelligences. Share what you know. It will make teaching and learning better for everyone.

And think about those individuals you know who are super smart. Maybe they'd seem less weird and better balanced had all their teachers allowed them to dance, draw, reflect, and develop their musical intelligences!

Recommended Reading

To learn more about how to prepare students for a career in music, read *Five Minds for the Future*, also by Howard Gardner (2006).

Self-Assessment Guide, Part IV:
Enhancing and Advancing the Profession

How to Use This Assessment Guide

Reflecting privately, or with the support of others, assess your current professional performance, or your preparation for the profession, along the continuum of responses provided in the chart (the numbered items correspond with the tips in the preceding section). There are no right answers; just be honest with yourself. When you are finished, your assessment might reveal needs and areas for further skill development.

You might also encourage a teacher, a friend, or a mentor to share with you how each perceives your professional work and compare and reflect together.

Informal self-assessment and evaluation are important endeavors for all professionals. If you frequently engage in reflective activities you should be well prepared for any outcomes of formal evaluation processes.

My preparation and/or professional performance skills indicate that I . . .	Strongly Disagree	Disagree	Neutral	Agree	Strongly Agree	No Opinion, No Response
45. advocate for the arts and their study.						
46. understand the background and needs of students and families in poverty.						
47. promote the benefits of music study with parents.						
48. focus on public relations to promote my program.						
49. seek out key community leaders for program support and recognition.						
50. value the contributions and support of school classified staff.						
51. participate in community activities.						
52. write grants to support my program.						
53. value, support, and contribute to the efforts of parent organizations.						

My preparation and/or professional performance skills indicate that I . . .	Strongly Disagree	Disagree	Neutral	Agree	Strongly Agree	No Opinion, No Response
54. prepare a high-quality written program to promote and document performances.						
55. effectively train volunteers and chaperones.						
56. address a variety of performance skills and standards in lessons.						
57. teach and reinforce proper audience etiquette.						
58. compensate and recognize the work of accompanists.						
59. understand the learning needs students of varied ages.						
60. cooperate, collaborate, and get along with others.						
61. engage the community.						
62. make ethical decisions.						
63. organize and work cooperatively with fundraisers.						
64. ask questions effectively.						
65. demonstrate pride and passion in professional work.						
66. promote and support quality music experiences for preschool students.						
67. address learning needs and teach to students' multiple intelligences.						

PART V

TIPS FOR PERSONAL GROWTH

Triumph is just the extra "umph" added to "try."

—Author unknown

Before we can conquer the world, we must be able to conquer ourselves.

—Alexander the Great

The secret to getting ahead is getting started.

—Mark Twain

Do a little more than you're paid to
Give a little more than you have to
Try a little harder than you want to
Aim a little higher than you think possible
And give a lot of thanks to God for
health, family, and friends.

—Art Linkletter

TIP 68

~

Have a Life Outside School and Spend Quality Time with Your Family

If you allow it, teaching music can become a 24-hour-a-day job. But that isn't a lifestyle that is healthy for anyone. You need balance and quality time with family and friends to spend on hobbies and activities unrelated to music. Failure to achieve balance can lead to burnout and worse, the loss of your family and friends.

You will never finish every project or find enough time to practice every selection. Do your best in the time allotted, and then go home. Exercise, meditate, walk the dog, read a good book, eat dinner with the family, go shopping, work in the garden, take a nap, or do whatever helps get your mind off the day and allows you to relax. Take time to recharge for the next day. Make sure you get enough sleep each night.

Dennis was a workaholic. Cheryl, his wife, knew that when they married. She didn't share Dennis' passion for music but tried to appreciate and tolerate it. They had two adorable children. Together, they had decided that Cheryl would stop teaching and be a stay-at-home mom while the kids were little. In their seventh year of marriage, Dennis became director of bands at Homestead High School and threw himself into meeting the new demands of this prestigious job, which was a 30-minute commute from his home. He left for work before 6:00 a.m. and often returned home after 10:00 p.m. Even on weekends, Dennis was preoccupied with his job and often away on band business. He never noticed the growing distance and wall that emerged in his relationship with Cheryl. He resented her constant nagging. So he often found it easier to stay at work and be free of her constant demands.

You might imagine how that scenario further develops. All too often, the marriage eventually disintegrates and dissolves. Young children's lives and sense of security are put at-risk. The hopes and dreams of two intelligent and competent individuals are shattered. Neither will ever completely recover from the hurt, guilt, shame, and failure of the relationship. Both will spend years attempting to recover financial losses and re-establish their quality of life.

Guard against making similar mistakes. Balance the demands of your professional and private life. The interests of your family should always come first. Spend quality time with your spouse and kids. Take care of your parents. Show appreciation for those in your life who love you the most and will be there for you long after the tenure of any job has expired.

TIP 69

~

Don't Smoke

For decades, Americans have heard antismoking messages. Everyone knows the dangers. Research clearly links smoking to cancer. It's dirty. It's no longer cool. Music teachers are well-educated people. They work with students of an age where smoking can result in school suspensions or be an illegal act. They model poor choices. Yet far too many music teachers continue to smoke.

One day when Roger was attempting to teach chromatic fingerings to a class of beginning saxophone players, Isabel said, "Mr. Rogers, your breath smells." Embarrassed, and realizing that his sense of smell no longer provided self-awareness, he decided to quit, cold turkey. For years, Roger's habit had been the subject of gossip among his high school instrumentalists and their parents, especially when he had to sneak behind the football stadium for a quick smoke. Most students laughed about his poor example. It took Isabel's brutal but innocent comment to get his attention.

If you smoke, quit. It wastes time and money. Set a good example. Join a support group and work with others who are trying to quit. Don't offend nonsmokers by exposing your bad habit in front of them.

Don't smoke!

Keep Fit

You can practice for hours to acquire the most advanced levels of musicianship, but you won't be an effective teacher for long unless you have a strong, healthy body. Effective music teachers are capable of many hours of productive, unrelenting work. They rarely miss school because of illness. They sleep well, eat a balanced diet, drink moderately, and engage in some form of regular exercise. There is no doubt that people who are fit move up the professional ladder faster than those who are not.

Music teachers who are physically fit tire less easily after long days, appear happier, and suffer less from depression. They also have the energy to cook dinner for their families, coach soccer teams, attend evening activities, and become involved in their community.

Invest in a good pair of athletic shoes. Walk or run. It's cheap. Many runners value private time for thinking while jogging. Others enjoy group runs. Enroll in yoga or kickboxing. Find your special time of day for exercise. Do what works for you.

Just do something!

TIP 71

~

Eat a Balanced Diet

Researchers and statisticians have identified childhood obesity as a national crisis. Without a determined effort to reverse current trends, the life expectancy of today's children could become shorter than that of their parents. Spend any time in the hallways of our nation's schools and you'll observe that the problem isn't exclusively the kids'; it's also shared by many adults. Most of us simply have too much available to eat. Our country has junk food everywhere and citizens whose lifestyles lack an adequate amount of exercise.

Develop a personal meal plan that fits your unique needs and includes the daily requirements from the basic food groups. Eat in moderation and take a walk or get some form of exercise after meals. Stay out of the refrigerator and eat healthy snacks.

Music teachers are often compulsive individuals by nature. History indicates that musicians also have a strong tendency to be possessed by addictions. But musicians are also well educated, should learn from others' mistakes, and know enough to exercise willpower and care for their body.

Model good eating habits for your students. Don't allow snacks in the music room. Avoid selling junk food and candy during fundraisers. Eliminate stops at fast food restaurants during music field trips. Don't drink a sugar-filled soft drink in front of students. Make sure your students know that you get up each morning and make time to eat a healthful breakfast, the most important meal of the day.

Students must learn at an early age that successful musicians need healthy bodies. Authorities are warning that obesity could lead to higher incidents of diabetes, high blood pressure, heart disease, and respiratory problems. This subject is very sensitive, but critically important to our collective future welfare. Music teachers must join forces with healthcare professionals, parents, and other concerned leaders to address health issues and eating habits with their students. You have influence. They will listen and follow the lead of their role model.

TIP 72

~

Don't Miss School
Unless You Are Really Sick

Cheryl had 10 years of experience teaching middle school vocal music. Her primary responsibilities included directing two choirs. She did a competent job. But her principal had become frustrated that she would appear on the absent list the day following every concert. Cheryl's closest colleagues also knew she would miss. They had overheard her say she was planning a "mental health day."

Cheryl was in her early 30s and appeared by most standards to be quite healthy. Yet she felt she had the "rest" days coming as part of her sick leave. So she stayed at home, missing the opportunity to reflect on the performance with each ensemble when it was fresh in students' minds.

Cheryl's principal had caught on to the attendance pattern but knew the union would protect their member if she challenged the absences. So she inwardly fumed, especially on the days when she had to cover Cheryl's classes when there were no available substitutes.

When Cheryl became engaged and planned to be married the next summer, a move to another city became imminent. But her efforts to find another teaching position met with rejection, despite her experience and competent performance in the classroom. Prospective employers learned during reference checks about her peculiar attendance record when it seemed she rarely exhibited symptoms of being sick. More consistent applicants got the jobs instead.

Unless you are really ill, don't abuse your sick leave policy. It is unethical to do so. Be a role model for your students. Take advantage of the best time to reflect on their performance.

~

Maintain a Positive Attitude

Don't leave for work with a bad attitude. There will be plenty of others who do, and without strong leaders to counter them, those selfish individuals' bad attitudes compound to create a negative work climate. Your attitude will impact your effectiveness. Don't expect to be promoted very far in the profession with a bad attitude. There is truth in the adage that says people don't care how much you know until they know how much you care.

In her second year as principal of Heritage Junior High School, Rita began discussions with her staff to adopt a middle school instructional philosophy instead of that of a traditional junior high school. But her ideas quickly met resistance. She became frustrated with comments like "I can't," "I'm afraid of," "I don't believe," "We've never done it that way," "We don't think that will work here," and so forth. So she began to commiserate with Donovan, her vocal music teacher, who expressed willingness to try. Donovan knew that by revamping the master schedule he could enroll more students in general music classes. He saw the proposal of the middle school concept as a good opportunity rather than bad.

Donovan had taught at Heritage for nearly 20 years. He had earned respect from students and parents because they knew he cared deeply about them. So when he began to verbalize his convictions about the need to address students' needs, people listened. Week by week, more colleagues agreed with his point of view and attitudes changed. Rita saw how important it was to confer with Donovan. Working closely together, Donovan helped her realize what positions she would need to give up to later accomplish her goals.

Together, their attitudes became contagious. The transformation took place over a three-year period, with Heritage emerging as a model middle school with a 90 percent student participation rate in the music program!

Every effective music teacher will encounter adversity and problems that may at times appear to be insurmountable. Those who don't encounter some obstacles experience very little change in their programs and probably aren't doing much. Draw upon your good attitude to persevere and to influence your students' learning about overcoming problems and challenges.

Help them learn from their mistakes. Not everyone will win the first chair seat or achieve a superior rating at every contest. Failure and disappointment are a part of life and should be seen as temporary. Don't get in a rut. Help students set realistic expectations and goals. Provide them several alternative approaches to achieve success. Focus on their strengths. Let them know you care. Model a good attitude.

The key to having a good attitude is the willingness to change.

—John Maxwell

TIP 74

~

Don't Overlook the Little Details

If your principal sets a deadline for the return of paperwork for all teachers, make sure yours is on time and completed with neatness and accuracy. Don't make excuses that you didn't have enough time before, during, or after school to complete the work. If there are 50 teachers and you are consistently one of a half-dozen that always miss deadlines, don't expect favors or your boss to be responsive to your needs.

If you invite a guest conductor to work with your orchestra, make sure you plan all the arrangements. Will the guest's travel costs be covered? If so, by whom? Will he or she need overnight accommodations? Who will make coffee the morning he or she arrives? Will he or she have a written plan and schedule to follow upon his or her arrival? Who will provide a score of the music to rehearse, and how far in advance will he or she receive it?

David was the new assistant band director put in charge of caring for the judges at the marching band invitational. He had attended high school where he now worked and participated in many invitationals. But as the activities of the day transpired, judges began grumbling to Gerald, the veteran band director, about the poor organization of the contest. No one was providing them with refreshments, the mileage rate on their travel vouchers was incorrect, and several of their tapes were mislabeled. David had neglected to call them together at the beginning of the contest to go over many of these details. Several of the judges were comparing the poor operation of the contest with others they had recently attended.

Both David and Gerald erred by overlooking the planning of the little details. David had experienced good contests, but he'd never had to think for himself of all the little details that create efficiency. Gerald had assumed David would know what to do and neglected planning with his rookie. Both were embarrassed. Gerald's frustration boiled over in anger. He exchanged harsh words with David and yelled at him for his poor performance. Judges left the event with a bad impression of the contest as well as the people.

Plan ahead. Don't assume every new teacher can envision all the little details previously handled by a veteran. Reflect and work for continuous improvement.

Together, David and Gerald sat down and wrote explanatory letters to the judges, apologized for their inefficient operation, and assured each that things would be better the following year. And true to their word, it was!

TIP 75

~

Don't Write Memos While Angry

Never send a memo or an e-mail that was written when you were angry or frustrated. It will come back to haunt you. It may be safe to write down what you are feeling, as writing can be a therapeutic process and help one organize thoughts and response to a problem. But don't hit the "send" key on the computer. It is always better to have a trusted colleague critique what you wrote. Phrase your comments in a professional manner. Buy time. Take a deep breath. Go run five miles. Put the nasty memo aside, cool off, read it when you've calmed down, and revise it. It is always best to personally discuss a problem or issue with another instead of engaging in a series of exchanges via e-mail.

Remember, e-mails and memos become public documents, so don't write anything that you wouldn't want the world to read. Don't burn your bridges. The person to whom you write a nasty memo today may be your boss tomorrow. Not all people share the same sense of humor, and once something has been written and sent, it has strange ways of showing up when you least want it. Be careful. Think twice before sending messages via the district computer network. If something warns you not to send it, don't!

Think positive thoughts!

~

Commiserate, But Be Careful Where

Caryn and Suzanne were both first-year instrumental music teachers in a large urban district. They became fast friends and frequently met for dinner to talk about the joys and challenges they were experiencing as rookie teachers.

As the school year progressed, they spent more and more time together venting. They talked about how their students appeared to lack motivation and discipline. They discovered they didn't know how to relate to kids living in drug-infested environments in extreme poverty. They didn't think the students had any interest in the music they'd selected to perform. Students didn't show them any respect. Everything they'd read in college about poor, tough inner-city schools was becoming an unpleasant reality. They experienced very little parent involvement or administrative support. They felt isolated. They agreed that if it weren't for the support they provided each other, each would have considered resigning and looking for another kind of work.

One night in March, at a popular family restaurant, they became so absorbed in their sharing and venting exchanges that their voices began to carry beyond the table where they were seated. Both commiserated about bad kids, bad parents, bad administrators, and bad working conditions. Everything in their professional lives seemed to be bad. Their experiences were also affecting their personal lives. As their venting continued, they were unaware that diners seated nearby could overhear their conversation.

Deep in their commiserations, neither Caryn nor Suzanne noticed the couple seated behind them stand up and prepare to leave. To their surprise, the gentleman approached them and said, "Excuse me for interrupting, but I just wanted you to know that my wife and I couldn't help but overhear your conversation. Both Ruth and I taught for 35 years in the schools you were talking about. We know those kids. We've been in the trenches. And would you both like a little free advice?"

"Well, yes, I guess so," said Suzanne.

"Certainly we would!" replied Caryn.

"For starters," the man began, "be careful where you're venting. You never know who might be listening. What if we had been parents of a student you were talking about or knew a student or the principal of your school? It's okay to vent. You need to vent. Just be careful where you do it."

"We're very sorry," Suzanne offered emphatically.

"No apologies necessary. Remember, both Ruth and I know what you are going through. Want another piece of advice?"

Both heads nodded positively.

"We kept overhearing how you both wished the kids would change, or their parents, or your principals. Based on 35 years experience, let me tell you this, it's not the kids who have to change. Kids are kids. Music students, particularly, are pretty much the same everywhere. There are just as many problems in the suburban schools—just different kinds with a more affluent genre of people. You are the ones who are going to have to change if you want to survive in the profession for your entire career."

The man paused to let that comment sink in, and then continued. "Think about it. You can't control how the students come to you. Their parents are sending you the best they have. But you can control how your react to your experiences and the people you work with. You want to make things better? Take the bull by the horns and do things for yourselves. You can't change the kids but you can change yourselves!"

At a loss for words, Caryn and Suzanne smiled and nodded in agreement.

"We wish you the best, ladies. Learn to be resilient and adapt. We hope you'll make it. Good luck!"

And with that, the veteran teachers were gone.

Back at Caryn's apartment, both reflected on the man's comments. They were shocked and embarrassed that their intimate commiserations had been overheard. But they soon began to focus on the wisdom of his advice. They spent the next several hours talking about their attitudes and planning strategies to counteract the stress they had been facing. They discussed what was within their realm of influence and what was not. They agreed to keep meeting but to vent in private. And they also agreed to support each other as they changed the way they approached their students and fulfilled their professional and personal expectations.

Caryn and Suzanne's dilemma is far too common. Music teachers become public figures within their community. Be careful what you say and where you say it. Select a safe place to share your experiences, feelings, and thoughts with a mentor or confidant. Don't apologize for needing to vent.

But listen while you vent, and act when you are given good advice.

~

Know When to Leave

Sadly, there may come a time when it is best to leave your position. Staying when conditions inhibit your growth or creative spirit will lead to cynicism and burnout. When things are tough, be careful as the old sayings warn, "Don't go barking up the wrong tree," and "Don't burn your bridges." Even more appropriate, "If you find yourself riding a dead horse, get off!" Nothing is more embarrassing than to still be playing when the song has ended.

There are times when every professional should move to a different position for new opportunities and challenges. Doing the same thing year after year creates conditions of the status quo syndrome. But situations may also develop outside your realm of control that could indicate time for a change. Such factors may include:

- limited resources and no indication of increases in the future
- cutbacks in district budgets that drastically limit arts programming
- continual lack of support for the arts from top administrative levels
- unmotivated and uncooperative colleagues in the music department
- lack of assistance to meet the growing demands from program growth.

Most of all, music teachers need to work for continuous improvement. Just as you would challenge and motivate a student to play music in an advanced method book instead of an intermediate level, music teachers need to stretch beyond their comfort zone and move to a more advanced position once they have accomplished all possible goals. Change can be difficult, but it is always constant. Music teachers must work so they are never stagnant.

~

Avoid the Dumb Mistakes
That Can Get You Fired

Read the papers or watch the evening news broadcasts and you'll frequently learn about a teacher accused of engaging in inappropriate relations or behavior with a minor. Music teachers are just as susceptible to unacceptable and illegal behaviors as their colleagues, and sometimes more so.

How you enjoyed your social time in college may no longer be appropriate in the more conservative environment of your school community. Even the way you dressed in college could violate professional dress codes in the real world. You may consider losing some tattoos or removing body piercings in order to prevent unnecessary attention to yourself in your new environment.

Under no conditions should you allow yourself to:

- engage in lewd conduct or sexual relations with a minor of either sex
- provide or partake of alcoholic beverages, drugs, or other illegal substances in the presence of minors. It isn't even good practice that adults see you drinking, especially if inebriated, in local pubs. Don't drink and drive. People will talk
- handle money or equipment without permission and policies that permit the practice. Never take anything that doesn't belong to you
- transport students in your motor vehicle without parent permission and authorization according to school policies
- falsify information or engage in other dishonest and deceitful practices
- violate the policies of the board of education

- be negligent or incompetent in fulfillment of professional duties
- engage in public or domestic violent behavior or other illegal acts.

Beginning teachers are vulnerable because they are often unaware of or unfamiliar with the established norms in their community. Open your eyes. Do what is morally right. If your conscience warns you not to do something, you probably should not.

Self-Assessment Guide, Part V:
Establishing and Enhancing Habits of Personal Growth

How to Use This Assessment Guide

Reflecting privately, or with the support of others, rate your professional performance, or your preparation for the profession, along the continuum of responses provided in the chart (the numbered items correspond with the tips in the preceding section). There are no right answers; just be honest with yourself. When you are finished, your assessment might reveal needs and areas for further skill development.

You might also encourage a teacher, a friend, or a mentor to share with you how they perceive your professional work and compare and reflect together.

Informal self-assessment and evaluation are important endeavors for all professionals. If you frequently engage in such activities you should be well prepared for any outcomes of formal evaluation processes.

My preparation and/or professional performance skills indicate that I . . .	Strongly Disagree	Disagree	Neutral	Agree	Strongly Agree	No Opinion, No Response
68. maintain balance between responsibilities at work and at home.						
69. avoid endangering health by smoking.						
70. maintain a regular personal fitness regimen.						
71. eat a balanced diet.						
72. have a good attendance record at work.						
73. display a positive attitude.						
74. focus on the little things that make a big difference.						
75. never react to situations in anger.						
76. vent and commiserate in private.						
77. know when to leave a dead-end job.						
78. avoid improper and immoral behaviors that could lead to dismissal.						

PART VI

~

TIPS FOR
PROFESSIONAL GROWTH

If you have a job without any aggravations, you don't have a job.

—Malcolm S. Forbes

When you do what you've always done, you get what you always got and you'll be where you've always been.

—Author Unknown

I use not only all the brains I have, but all I can borrow.

—Woodrow Wilson

TIP 79

~

Organize the Music Room and Office

Joel, an instrument repairman, spent his days traveling from school to school to fix instruments onsite and provide supplies as part of each school's contractual agreement with the local music store. As he made his rounds, he knew which teachers would be prepared for his visit and those who would not. Privately, Joel recognized that the cleanliness and organization of large rehearsal rooms, practice and storage areas, and directors' offices correlated positively with the overall organization and quality of music programs.

Joel's repair shop was full of equipment, yet lacked clutter. Everything had a place and his work area was clean. Joel knew where everything was located and daily spent time cleaning before going home, even though it wasn't part of his job. He couldn't understand how some of the professional music teachers he encountered could be such slobs and so disorganized.

In the music room, the teacher sets the tone. If you show little regard for the care of equipment, the students won't either. If you tolerate dust and clutter, expect more, not less. If your desk is messy, disorganized, and you never know where things are, don't chastise students who can't find their music. Set a good example and hold others accountable for their personal organization.

Joel was right. The best performing groups came from the schools where the director was organized, rooms were cleaned, painted, and maintained. The organization was visible to the eye upon first glance in the music room.

Visit schools. Observe how others keep house. Borrow ideas from those who have it together. Work continuously to be organized and on top of your game. Model best practice for your students.

TIP 80

~

Write Notes, Return Phone Calls, and Reply to E-Mail

Every teacher realizes that there is very little free time in a typical teaching day. And it seems there is always more to do, not less. But three daily routines should never be overlooked, whatever the work load may be: writing personal notes, returning phone calls, and replying to e-mail.

Every good mentor instills these habits in their protégé. The act of writing a personal thank you or congratulatory note demonstrates that you sincerely want to show gratitude, acknowledgment, or recognition for another's acts. Write three of them each day. Send a note to the nursing home director thanking him or her for the invitation to perform. Thank the superintendent and principal for their support. Thank special boosters for their assistance. Congratulate a colleague on a program they presented. Thank teachers for their support. Send notes to students commending their accomplishments, especially non-music activities. Recognize volunteer contributions. The returns on the investment of time and cost of stationary will be well worth it.

If a parent, student, vendor, or community patron calls and leaves a message, their reason for calling must have been important. Don't go home until every attempt has been made to return each of those calls. Don't procrastinate. Don't let important matters stall. The adage that "those who snooze will lose" is true. Capitalizing on opportunities that originate from phone calls requires immediate action, not some other time when you may get around to it. Of course, responding to e-mail, especially from parents, is just as important as a phone message. Check to see if your district has an expected or required response time for e-mail.

And when you make a telephone call and get placed "on hold," use the time to begin writing one of your three daily notes.

TIP 81

~

Learn How to Deal with
Conflict and Show Restraint

Because of a scheduling mistake originating in the athletic director's office, Jeannine and members of her marching band found the varsity team practicing on the football field one Thursday evening when it had been reserved for the band. Jeannine stopped the band and instructed her students to wait on the track until she could find Larry, the head coach, and resolve the obvious scheduling conflict.

But she didn't expect Larry's insensitivity and outburst. He told Jeannine there was no way he planned to vacate the field. Tomorrow's game was for the conference championship, and he was determined that nothing would interfere with this important practice. "You don't need the field, so go back inside to the band room and rehearse your tunes there!" he yelled with contempt.

"But Larry," Jeannine countered without raising her voice, "we have a state contest performance on Saturday, and we also need to practice under the lights. There isn't anyplace else to go. And anyway, we've reserved this field every Thursday night from 7 to 9 p.m."

"I don't give a damn about that, and I haven't got time to stand here and argue with you," Larry shouted to Jeannine's surprise. When she didn't leave, Larry's temper began to flare. He became enraged. Noticing the confrontation escalating, Jeannine's assistant stepped in for support. But Larry allowed the team to continue practicing, within earshot of their conversation, while he continued cursing and belittling Jeannine and the band program.

With restraint, Jeannine withdrew to avoid a scene that she thought would only escalate further out of control. She directed the band to a lighted parking lot and improvised as best she could while completing the evening's practice. She refrained from discussing the situation with her students.

The next morning, Jeannine demanded a grievance hearing with the principal, athletic director, her assistant, and Larry. The conference was held that afternoon after school. Calling upon all her training and experience, Jeannine knew a confrontational approach would not solve this conflict. So, when asked, she calmly voiced her viewpoint, expressed her needs, and described her feelings. Larry, on the other hand, continued to be demeaning and indignant toward Jeannine and her band. When his competitive temper flared and the cursing emerged, the principal stopped the mediation and issued a suspension against Larry. Jeannine was surprised by that outcome. She realized that a mutual resolution of differences with Larry would require much time. Most of all, she was proud of herself for showing restraint, sticking to the issues, standing strong, and displaying an attitude of cooperation willing to find a compromise. She was pleased when the principal complimented her for the ability to maintain composure and stated, "You really earned my respect today!"

This scenario happens all too often. If not a similar situation, perhaps it is an affront from an upset parent whose son or daughter wasn't selected for a first-chair position. Or a fight that develops between two headstrong students. Regardless, no matter how you may want to avoid it, music teachers frequently find themselves involved in or expected to mediate conflict situations. It is an unavoidable part of the job.

Take a class or workshop in conflict resolution. Learn how to manage conflicts in order to minimize risks, maximize benefits, and increase personal and professional growth. Know yourself and your conflict resolution style. Are you an avoider, an accommodator, a compromiser, a competitor, or a negotiator?

Teachers must learn that they can't avoid or do away with conflict. Instead, they must learn to handle and defuse it in ways that produce growth and constructive solutions. Acknowledge others' feelings. Learn to treat others with respect, listen, focus on issues rather than emotions or people, and use "I" statements that diffuse the energy of the situation and help express feelings. Personal feelings that are allowed to fester during a mediation session will only remerge later in another conflict.

It is possible, with successful mediation, to build a close relationship with someone who has mistreated you. Like it or not, you'll be cast as a mediator between students and parents. And like Jeannine, you'll sometimes become a participant. Be steady. Always work to make things better and prevent incidents and circumstances from being blown out of proportion.

Discussion Questions

How do you handle conflict?

    Do you avoid it?
    Do you accommodate it or give in to others?
    Do you compete to get your way?
    Do you compromise?
    Do you collaborate?

There are times and situations where any choice might be the most appropriate. However, everyone has a dominant style. Identify your strengths and weaknesses. Study conflict management skills. You'll benefit from this training when you need to resolve conflicts with coaches and in every other conflict as well.

Always Show Restraint

High-maintenance parents often test your patience. So do their kids. When you have to discipline their child, expect to receive a call or confrontation. If they don't get their way, they'll argue, try to intimidate, threaten, or do whatever it takes to get satisfaction. No wonder their kids often act the same. An apple doesn't fall far from the tree.

Most veteran music teachers have experienced angry cursing parents, threats, and people who they discover to be unreasonable, irrational, or "just plain crazy." When people lose control, they raise their voice, throw temper tantrums, point their fingers, and sometimes curse. Others will cry. They love to cause a public scene. If you find yourself suddenly confronted and verbally attacked, never respond. Stay calm. Move toward other people or send a reliable student for assistance. Don't blow off steam in front of others because everything you say will become gossip and might later be used against you.

You do not have to tolerate cursing or threats. Once this happens, person-to-person or via the phone, calmly state that if the conversation is to continue, participants must refrain from using foul language, slinging insults, or making threats. If the problem persists, calmly state that you are ending the conversation and request the agitator schedule a follow-up meeting with you when and if self-control can be gained. Document your conversation and file an incident report with your principal. You may need a witness at the follow-up conference.

As much as you may be tempted, you cannot lower yourself to the agitator's level. Show restraint. You cannot engage in inappropriate behavior. Hold your tongue. Be mindful of your body language. Sometimes, you simply need to allow the person to vent without responding. Focus on issues, not personalities.

Let the other person play the role of the fool. You are the professional.

Discussion Questions

1. How would others describe your composure under pressure?
2. When you are nervous, does it show?
3. What lessons do children learn from adults that maintain composure and from those parents that do not?
4. Can you recall examples of music teachers that always seemed capable of maintaining their cool?
5. How well do you handle surprise questions from the media?

Furthermore

Brainstorm a list of celebrities, politicians, sports figures, and other notables in the public eye who you feel consistently demonstrate constraint under pressure.

1. Discuss what happens in the media when an individual loses composure.
2. Discuss training strategies and special considerations that music teachers must employ, not only for themselves, but that they should teach to students to control nerves and maintain composure in performance venues.

TIP 82

~

Prepare Your Students
and Yourself for the Future

In his book, *Five Minds for the Future* (2006), psychologist Howard Gardner identifies cognitive abilities and capacities that will gain individuals an advantage in a global society:

- the disciplinary mind: the mastery of major schools of thought (including science, mathematics, and history) and at least one art form.
- the synthesizing mind: the ability to integrate ideas from different disciplines or spheres into a coherent whole and to communicate that integration to others.
- the creating mind: the capacity to uncover and clarify new problems, questions, and phenomena.
- the respectful mind: an awareness of and appreciation for differences among human beings.
- the ethical mind: the fulfillment of one's responsibilities as a worker and a citizen.

Accomplished musicians possess strengths in each. A future that appreciates and values the disciplined training and thinking skills of creative musicians is at hand. The disciplined study of music integrates the sciences, math, and history. Reading and performing music requires an ability to quickly process huge amounts of stimuli, to make sense of it all, and express it in a new and enlightening manner for others. Musicians are by nature creative people, willing to challenge the rules, respectful of diversity, and welcoming of those from other cultures. A musician with an ethical mind conceives responsibilities at work and with other human beings in ways that contribute consistently to what is just and virtuous in society.

Seize the opportunities described by Gardner. Teach what is really important, not just what is needed to pass a standardized test or win first place at a contest. Help students identify role models that epitomize the skilled, disciplined, and creative minds needed for the future. Initiate changes that motivate students to be better than good, but instead to acquire disciplined skills and greater levels of knowledge than students anywhere else in the world. Those who are prepared for their future will thrive.

Discussion Questions

1. What will it require for those students who are now in first grade to become successful as adults? What will the consequences be for them if they fail?
2. What opportunities will emerge for music education in the global world of high technology, advanced sciences, computers, robots, instant communication, and increased diversity among cultures? What opportunities might be missed if music educators do not cultivate the five minds for the future?

TIP 83

~

Know Your Audience

Nathan and his marching band staff were glum and dejected following a halftime performance at which the rival Panther Marching Band received a standing ovation from the crowd while theirs did not. "How could our home crowd be so rude to our kids?" they said as they fumed at the concession stand.

How could they? Why did they? The reality was that the audience simply appreciated and responded to a more entertaining halftime show. Nathan had trouble understanding and accepting that reality.

Nathan and his staff, like many others who felt compelled to be involved in the state marching competitions, thought it was best to work on one show throughout most of the marching season. They would routinely rehearse and drill the same music and field maneuvers each week. They emulated the major drum and bugle corps that traveled the country every summer dazzling their faithful followers with precision and musicality. And despite their students' younger age and varied commitment levels, they pushed on in attempt to reach the same levels of perfection as the drum corps.

But the home crowd had tired of their show. They didn't have an interest in or an appreciation for their style. There were mumblings throughout the bleachers. "Why can't our band play some rousing music and entertain like that band?" was typical of the comments being made as the crowd stood and applauded while the Panthers left the field.

Nathan and his staff were out of touch. They were surrounded by loyal band parents who held them in the highest regard. But they were afraid to criticize. Moreover, their ranks were dwindling as students opted for other activities and sports during the marching season. The band was gradually decreasing in size. Students and parents had grown tired of the daily after school rehearsal schedule, the home and away Friday night games, and Saturday contest. Fewer and fewer shared the commitment or enjoyed the thrill of performing for the unappreciative home crowd. Increasing numbers rebelled against the concept of being a competition show band and chose activities that provided an acceptable alternative to marching band.

Nathan had unwittingly gone along with the traditions that had been established in the band program when he accepted his job. He never bothered to learn about the football crowd. He was immune from hearing their comments. But following this embarrassment, he set about getting better in tune.

- Football fans couldn't understand and didn't like it that band members never played the fight song to support their team during third quarter
- Fans thought the band was too rigid and militaristic in their parade marching style
- Fans could not relate to the music selected for competition shows. Nathan also learned that a high percentage of his students couldn't either
- Fans lost interest when the halftime began, and it took three or four minutes to set the sideline percussion instruments while the band warmed up on the field
- Fans wanted to see a different show each week and to be entertained
- Fans expected a Friday night pageant, support, and cooperation between the band, cheerleaders, and the team. What they were observing seemed disjointed.

Nathan and his staff reflected and spent time after the season ended revamping their program. They didn't abandon the corps style competition show, but they decided to teach other marching styles as well. They prepared several differing shows for the next year, limited the number of competitions, and revised the daily rehearsal schedule so students had more free time. They continued to focus on teaching and realized they would need to educate the football crowd about what they were viewing in halftime shows. They developed a plan to have a pep group always available and responsive during key moments throughout the game. The band was instructed to get on the field differently and much more rapidly for halftime shows than they did for competitions. Nathan and his staff borrowed ideas from college marching bands to add more pageantry to the Friday night community event. The kids were allowed to have some fun.

And they did. And the crowds noticed. Eventually they showed their enthusiasm and appreciation on their feet at each game. Never again was the home band embarrassed.

TIP 84

~

Don't Procrastinate

Don't put things off that you can and must complete today. Sounds like your mother's advice? Maybe so, and it is a key bit of advice for music teachers.

Like other educators and leaders, music teachers must make dozens of decisions each day that keep their programs focused and classes moving forward. But when the teacher is absent, or even worse, working but not making necessary decisions, activities stall. Think of the things that only you can do or decide and how many people would be affected if you didn't take action. When the lead marcher suddenly halts, everyone behind stops and a pile-up occurs.

How many times have you attended meetings where important issues or questions were discussed only to be tabled, referred to committee, or dropped altogether? Remember the feelings of frustration? Don't let that happen at your music department faculty or parent group meetings. People resist investing their time and energy to discuss important issues if they think nothing will happen. Sometimes, the leader simply has to make a decision to keep things moving.

Don't keep the kids waiting while you ponder what selections will become part of the next program. Don't delay arranging details of the Saturday contest because students and parents won't have time to arrange their schedules. Don't put off completing the paperwork that your principal expects the next day. Do so, and it is almost certain a crisis will develop that keeps you from getting it done when you'd planned.

Procrastinators are indecisive or lazy. Neither is a descriptor you want people to think fits you.

~

Avoid the "Geek" Stereotype

.

What is a "geek?" What is the connotation of that term, or others like "nerd," "jock," or "yokel?" Do students at your school think of you in terms like these? Anyone who ever watched the movie *Animal House* will remember the portrayal of the jocks as cool and popular and the nerds as social outcasts.

It seems to be a common rite of passage that high school students associate themselves and their classmates with a clique of some kind. Peer pressure often influences and dictates how students dress, talk, and spend their free time. Most students want to be part of the in-group and will say and do whatever is necessary to gain attention and stature. Kids can be cruel and merciless with those they feel do not conform to the popular fads and patterns of behavior.

So what can a music teacher do? How is it that some professionals successfully recruit participants from all social groups within the school while others gain interest and retain but few? Could it be personality? Is it how one looks, dresses, acts, and develops relationships?

Look in the mirror. If you look like a geek, you'll attract those who gravitate toward geeks. If you don't like what you see, get a makeover. If your interests are so narrow that you can't talk about anything other than music, you'll find it hard to engage those whose interests are more widespread and worldly. Know what is happening in the mainstream of youth culture. Read their magazines and be familiar with what they watch on television. Know what kind of music interests them and the movies they enjoy. Show interest in students as individuals and talk with them about their activities outside the music room.

Students are attracted to what they like and what they think is popular. Mix with everyone, socialize, and advocate the benefits of involvement in music and being well rounded. When students perceive their music teachers to be of the real world, they will enroll in their classes and participate in performing groups without fear of ridicule from their friends.

~

Build a Team within the Music Department

There are too many instances of controversy among staff members in school music programs. Everyone seems to know someone who works in an environment where jealousy rules between the instrumental and vocal department, where teachers won't speak to each other, and where there is a lack of communication from person to person and school to school.

To build a team, it helps to have experience being part of a team. If you find yourself as the newest member of the music staff, get involved and work to establish your credibility with the veterans. Earn their respect and their trust. Carry your fair share of the workload and don't let the others down. Don't engage in gossip or take sides if there are factions within the department.

But if it becomes apparent there is no productive team concept within the music department, take a leadership role in developing one. Learn how to collaborate, utilize conflict management skills, act professionally, be ethical in your actions, and if all fails and conditions appear they can never improve, know when to leave.

Seek help from your principal, supervisors, superintendent, or other persons of authority who can help establish expectations for a music department team. Request regular meetings. Keep minutes. Focus on what is best for the entire department and all music students. No matter the size of the district, it is best when there is a unified music department, one booster group, sharing, mutual support and respect.

Imagine if the oboists couldn't get along with the violists or the tenors with the altos. Everyone knows the fickle temperament of a prima donna.

The effective music teacher goes to great lengths to resolve conflicts and build a team within the ensemble.

Likewise, effective music teachers must sometimes go to great strides to build a team within the music department. They must stand up and lead. There will never be quality outcomes when there is dissonant harmony within the music department.

What Would You Do If?

You were a veteran fifth-grade instrumental music teacher responsible for recruitment. In any given year, your data shows that you start 120 students, only to promote them to your middle school where Dave, your colleague, is so ineffective that he turns so many off that nearly 50 percent of your recruits quit. Students come back to see you and complain about band. They ask you to be their teacher again. The situation bothers you tremendously and you feel powerless to change it.

Dave is manipulative and devious. He shows no desire to improve. He is not a team player. He talks about his retirement all the time, but that milestone is six years away. He is a golf buddy of the middle school principal. You don't think the principal would listen if you made him aware of the poor retention from fifth to sixth grade.

What options might you pursue? How do you seek help?

~

Always Make Your Principal Look Good

This tip should seem obvious, but too many educators, including music teachers, don't appear to get it. Instead of addressing issues and concerns about their boss in a professional manner behind closed doors, they publicly air their grievances and frustrations without regard to who may hear. Without regard, they talk too freely about sensitive matters with parents and even students. They waste time gossiping and participating in the "gripevine" when their energies could be better invested working harder to make things better.

"Sure," you say, "but I'm working for the world's most ineffective principal!"

Regardless, what follows are some time honored courtesies and gestures that will go a long way toward building a positive rapport with any administrator:

- Make sure the principal is informed about any problem you have encountered with a student immediately—always before you go home for the day. You don't want the principal to learn about a serious issue from a parent. Make sure your viewpoint is heard first
- Keep the principal up-to-date about all music booster activities. Always extend an invitation to meetings. Provide a heads-up when you sense any issue brewing
- Develop a schedule of regular performances and special programs at the beginning of each year. Anticipate that this schedule will change with-

out much notice. Be prepared for impromptu assemblies and requests for performance groups to play without much warning. Be supportive and cooperative when asked at the last minute to "save the day"

- Always list the principal's name in concert programs, and make sure a copy is shared in advance. Always acknowledge your principal's attendance at programs and invite him or her to say a few words
- Teaching music is not a nine-to-five job. Realize that you will need to be at school before and after your colleagues. Don't complain about how much extra time you devote to your job
- Don't be a whiner during staff meetings or talk about the principal in the hallways afterward. Compliments go further than complaints. It is fine to acknowledge challenges but better to suggest solutions rather than celebrate problems
- Provide your principal with special announcements about the music program or information for newsletters and Web pages. Write a weekly "good news" e-mail about a student's learning and success. Principals are always working to promote their school. Become the principal's right-hand person with public relations
- Be resourceful. No principal has enough money in the budget for everything you might need
- If you are an itinerant teacher, keep each principal and assistant principal completely informed of activities of the entire music program
- Think, act, and dress professionally at all times.

TIP 88

~

Observe Each Other

Beth's principal, admittedly, had minimal background and experiences in music. He didn't know what to look for when observing and completing her annual evaluation, and he made that clear to Beth. But wisely, he did recommend and make accommodations for her to spend time observing her music colleagues in the district and elsewhere.

Music teachers know the benefits of playing and listening to recitals. Listeners can gain many insights from performers that can be applied to their own work. But the performer also benefits from the preparation, sharing, and self-satisfaction during the recital.

Yet, music teachers rarely take time to observe and learn from each other. Some would say they never have any free time. But those who become most effective find it anyway. They also seek help from principals and request opportunities to learn from their colleagues.

Take advantage of your planning time, lunch, or recess breaks, even if it's only five minutes and step in a colleague's classroom to observe. It doesn't always have to be a music classroom where you can gather your best ideas. Observe how others interact with and manage their students. Identify ways in which it is obvious that they are engaged and learning.

People tend to clean up and organize when they know company is coming. They want to create a good impression. The same is true when a colleague comes to observe. The music room becomes a little tidier and the lesson given more consideration and planning. The host reaches performance mode. And if you are effective, you learn to approach *each* day as if it were a performance. You never know who might stop by to observe.

TIP 89

~

Guard against Burnout

It's unlikely to suffer the effects of burnout if you've never been on fire teaching music in the first place. There are individuals like that—not many—but everyone must admit they exist. They are most likely to be the complainers and whiners. "This job is too much. The kids won't practice. Their parents won't help. I have too many classes to teach. I don't have enough time to plan. The paperwork is overwhelming. I'm tired and feel burned out." It is more probable that teachers echoing these statements have lost their passion. They are bored and unmotivated to do anything more than what is minimally required.

But it's those on the other end of the continuum who are most likely to experience the effects of burnout. The superstars never know when or how to say no. They volunteer for all the school committees. Principals seek them out when they need something done right. They are the high energy, high achievers, and everyone knows it. They are ready, willing, and capable of doing anything. They accomplish what few others can do. Even within a music department, there are acknowledged high achievers and others who do not pull their weight. It's the stress that builds from pulling slackers along as they drag anchor that leads to burnout. Like running a race, one can only go so far for so long with weights around the ankles until exhaustion takes over.

Don't volunteer and do things that others can and should do. If you are a supervisor, don't ask the superstars to complete all the routine tasks that may be necessary from lesser colleagues. Don't apply unnecessary pressure on yourself or others. Delegate responsibilities. Avoid allowing superstars to engage in unimportant work. Empower students to complete less essential tasks that consume time and energy of high achievers.

Superstar teachers will never experience burnout when they feel valued and important. They are task oriented and continuously motivated by the work and opportunities around them. Don't allow yourself or others to be consumed by unimportant tasks. Balance the workload. Share the responsibilities. Get out, if necessary, when the conditions cannot be controlled.

TIP 90

~

Read

Reading is fundamental. It is a goal of every teacher that children learn to read and to enjoy a lifetime of reading. Music teachers also desire their students learn to read music. To set the best example, read. Let others see you read.

Music teachers must read the journals of the leading professional associations. They must understand laws. Read magazines about current events. Read the newspapers. Reading books expands the mind and enables the learner to gain new insights. Read for enjoyment and relaxation.

Just like making time for fitness, music teachers must find time to read. Share good titles with colleagues, and encourage others to share their insights from books with you.

Readers are more inquisitive, knowledgeable, and well rounded than their colleagues who are "too busy" to read. Readers have thoughts to share in conversations. They think more critically. Readers practice what they preach. They model adult learning. They become the leaders of their school.

TIP 91

∼

Give Professional Presentations

Not only should music teachers join state and national professional associations, but they should also get involved, volunteer, chair a committee, and share an idea or best practice with others at a professional workshop or conference. Share what you've learned. Learn from others. Be authentic. Perform!

Effective music teachers know that they learn more about playing an instrument when teaching it to someone else. Likewise, preparing to present, writing a speech, and preparing a concurrent session for a professional conference are all valuable learning experiences. You really master the material when you teach it to others. Learn to do it well. Share authentic experiences and stories. Help people learn from your experience and implement your ideas in their work.

It is flattering to be asked to present, and it is a professional compliment when someone else "borrows" your ideas for their work setting. Many of the best ideas and practices in schools are those that have been shared and passed around through numerous professional conferences.

Do it! Submit a proposal today. Everyone has something to share. Most professional associations have their requests for proposals (RFPs) online. Let the learning begin!

TIP 92

~

Find a Mentor

Mentors love learning and growing. They also love what the protégé can become. There is passion in effective mentoring partnerships, and great mentors recognize the vitality of communicating all they know to a willing protégé.

Teaching is hard work. Teaching music often casts one in the school and community spotlight. The training from college and university preparatory programs is simply not enough to prepare a master teacher for the transition to the real world of work. To support a successful entry into the profession or a change to a new position, many school districts provide mentoring programs. They have been developed to help "rookies" learn and grow in a safe environment, avoid the traps, and develop strategies to meet new challenges. All teachers need a mentor. Effective music teachers, whatever their experience level, have trusted mentors who have guided, nurtured, supported, and listened with compassion and devotion throughout their career—and they continue to rely upon them.

Mentoring is a partnership. It requires a time commitment. Giving and learning are shared between mentor and protégé. An effective partnership is characterized by generosity, truth, trust, continuous communication, love of learning, acceptance, patience, devotion, passion, love, interpersonal relationship, courage, resiliency, and positive attitudes.

The success of the mentoring partnership depends upon both the mentor and the protégé. It can hang on the rapport that is developed in the first encounters between them. Both need to be willing to commit to building a strong relationship, free of anxiety or fear. The protégé needs to search for the master teacher, one that is receptive to learning, sharing, teaching, and reflecting. Once compatibility, rapport, and trust are established in the partnership, both will work to draw the best out of each other.

Fear is a barrier to learning. Find a mentor. Learn together. As partners, both will enjoy making music in their communities.

TIP 93

~

Perform

Can students be expected to learn skills and model good habits when their physical education teacher is grossly overweight? How does a teacher in that state of health set an example and motivate students to excel on physical fitness tests? How much different is the music teacher who can't, or won't, perform? Neither are good role models for kids.

Students learn best to play an instrument or sing when they hear their teacher do the same. Master teachers have worked to acquire the desired vocal sound, technique, and tone on all the instruments for which they have responsibility. They routinely demonstrate those good habits, form, and style to their students. Much about learning to play an instrument well is gleaned from listening to a variety of accomplished performers, and one of those individuals should be a student's teacher.

Many music teachers become so absorbed in their daily routine that they neglect setting aside time for themselves and for practicing. Before long, the embouchure becomes weak, the technique sloppy, and it becomes increasing difficult to perform. The adage that "If I miss a week's practice, I notice—if I miss two week's practice, my audience notices" becomes a reality.

Practice. Teach private lessons. Volunteer to sing or play in church. Start a community ensemble for adults. Do whatever it takes to sustain your performance skills. Never allow yourself to succumb to intimidation or feelings of inferiority. Be a good role model for students.

TIP 94

~

Continually Improve
Your Stage Presence

Sylvia was the envy of every teacher at Lincoln High School, but she didn't know it. Her colleagues recognized her poise and stage presence when speaking during her choral concerts. Without any natural striking, personal features, Sylvia drew immediate attention when dressed impeccably in concert black attire. She was a master of timing. Her stride onto the stage was at just the right pace, her smile lit up the auditorium, and her voice needed no amplification. When she spoke, her voice conveyed warmth, confidence, and authority. Her statements were timed with just enough words, always grammatically correct, and free of annoying colloquialisms. When Sylvia spoke, people listened.

Sylvia's voice and presence also commanded attention at staff meetings. She spoke only when appropriate. When she did, her points were focused and made with few words. She was never condescending. She never whined. She modeled professionalism. Her warm smile, eye contact, and vocal inflections captured the attention of everyone.

What her colleagues didn't know was how Sylvia's training had prepared her for her role. As a youngster, she was taught how to walk to the piano, bow, and accept applause at recitals. If she was to speak, the words were scripted in advance. She learned when it was appropriate to smile and how to look into an audience, conveying an image that she was looking at and speaking to each individual. Her projection skills were taught by her voice teacher. Routinely with her teachers, she reviewed and analyzed audio and video tapes of her performances, always striving for perfection. She became her own best critic. She aspired to the highest standards. And she never stopped reflecting and striving for continuous improvement. She knew that her stage presence, and that of her students, were an integral part of a quality choral program, and she never walked onto a stage unprepared.

Look in the mirror. What do you see? A presence like Sylvia's or something less? Are you comfortable speaking in front of audiences? Would others describe you as unflappable? How do you sound on tape? Do you make your points effectively or do you sputter and stumble like many athletes and politicians on television interviews?

Set high standards for yourself. Pay attention to your hair, avoid glare from glasses, and wear clothes that fit and enhance your presence. Think about what you should say, who must be acknowledged, and practice speaking in the mirror before the program. Record all performances, reflect, and use them to improve the performance of students and yourself. Actors and actresses work continuously to perfect their art. So must you.

Concertgoers should expect quality music and are quick to show their appreciation when performers do well. The music teacher sets the tone. Don't forget to plan and prepare for one of the most integral parts of every performance.

~

Collaborate and Network

Teaching is a challenging business, and to be successful, educators need to work together, share ideas, work to solve common problems, and share best practices. There is an historical perception that music programs are structured around competitions and entertainment. But it must be much more. Competition can be healthy and must be structured so that students learn to compete against an established standard and their own ability to achieve, not at the expense of others. Music will always entertain, but that is not the sole purpose.

But countering historic perceptions ingrained in a community can be hard. Music teachers need to work together, intra- and inter-districts, develop a collegial network, share successes and failures, promote best practices, and advocate for and promote the profession.

Teachers who work in isolation or stoke their egos at the expense of others drag anchor on those who work as collaborators. There is no *I* in team.

TIP 96

~

Avoid the Status-Quo Syndrome

If you continue to do what you've always done, you shouldn't be upset if you get the same results. That's a twist on a wise old saying, and it should ring as true for music teachers as anyone else. Pity the person who teaches 30 years in the same room doing the same lessons and programs year after year in the very same way. There are those who teach for 30 years possessing as much enthusiasm on the last day as their first. Others seem to repeat what they learned the first year 29 times afterwards—growing more cynical as time passes by.

Doing things the very same way is what causes the status quo syndrome. It is quite possible to teach in the same room or school for 30 years, learning, growing, reinventing, and continuously improving performance. Those individuals love learning. They have dreams and aspirations and are intrinsically motivated to excel. They look for and accept new challenges. They have an ability to supersede limitations that might exist within their organizational setting and change paradigms. They avoid situations and people that exhibit acute symptoms of the status quo. They realize that change is constant, good, and necessary for growth and advancement.

Don't fall into a rut. Marching band shows don't all have to look the same or follow the same style as other schools in the state. Avoid having programs on the same Friday night of the month, year after year. Don't sing the same songs each year in general music classes. Dare to be different. If you do teach the same classes, find a way to put a new twist on the objectives. Stay fresh. Learn something you didn't know before and enthusiastically share it with your students.

The same thinking year after year, and interacting only with those who think like you, are surefire ways to ensure you'll acquire the status quo syndrome. Meet new people, consider other perspectives, read, and share with others. Look around you. See what happens to those who lose their passion, commitment, and emotional connection to their work. Don't let that happen to you.

~

Improve Your Leadership Skills

Are leaders born or do they acquire their skills through life experiences? The literature is filled with books on this topic. It contains much more than typical music teachers need or want to know. But music teachers must realize that they are leaders and continuously work to improve their leadership skills. More than their colleagues in other disciplines, music teachers are leaders because they continually communicate their students' importance and potential. They have influence. Effective music teachers help their students acquire an intrinsic sense of worth. Attempting to create a sense of meaning solely with extrinsic motivators is flawed. Teach the whole person. Care for your students and create opportunities that enable students to see their potential for themselves.

Like all leaders assuming a new position, music teachers can benefit from a simple outline of the progressive levels of leadership. Read John Maxwell's *Leadership 101*. In this bestselling book, he lists the levels of leadership as:

1. Position.
2. Permission.
3. Production.
4. People development.
5. Personhood.

When first hired for a teaching position, new teachers find themselves at the position level. Unfortunately, some never progress further. They have a title, become complacent, fall into a rut, assume they have "arrived," and arrogantly fail to do anything with the title. They wonder why they can't make things happen, people don't like them, and their programs never improve.

Maxwell points out that leaders must progress naturally through the five levels, warning not to skip a level. That is the mistake Jose made!

Jose thought he had arrived when, at age 23; he was selected to become the director of bands at Union High School. He was hired August 10 and classes were scheduled to begin in less than three weeks. His predecessor had given no indication that he would retire before the start of the school year. An outstanding student and leader in college, Jose's ego became inflated when he won this job. Most of his peers had been unsuccessful in finding work. Quickly, Jose threw himself into making preparations, selecting music, and writing marching band drills.

On paper, Jose looked great. His resume and experiences had given him an edge over other candidates. He appeared fully qualified to fulfill the duties outlined on his job description. But in reality, this was the first professional experience in his life where Jose was completely on his own and responsible for his decisions.

In a rush to make up for time he felt had been lost over the summer months, Jose made his fateful mistake. He failed to gain permission from his students and parents to become their new leader. Instead, he immediately began expecting results, a third-level outcome—skipping level 2. Because his selection of music and marching styles were vastly different from his predecessor, his students revolted in September. Several seniors quit. Morale of the band had never been so low. Jose's efforts were ineffective, and frustrations erupted after the band failed to achieve a qualifying rating for state competition at their annual invitational contest. Jose's mentor then stepped in and helped him learn the importance of building relationships with those he needed to lead.

There is no doubt that Jose was prepared for the first level of leadership. He was bright. He was a very competent and skilled musician. Unfortunately, he was never given enough time to allow students and parents to come to that observation for themselves. In retrospect, Jose learned that he needed to assure his students and their parents that he did have the necessary training and skills to do his job. They had become accustomed to years of excellence during Mr. Edwards' tenure, and many had difficulty accepting and acclimating to the youthful enthusiasm and changes that Jose brought to the band program. After his mentor got him to slow down and reflect, Jose realized that he had skipped two important levels of leadership development.

Once a music teacher has been hired and spent adequate time building interpersonal relationships with all constituencies, solidifying permission to lead, much like friendships develop or husbands and wives establish themselves as couples, the teacher can eventually move up to the third level, production. Couples start families at this level, and music teachers and their students begin to realize the results and benefits of their work together. Progress is made, results are data driven, and improvement is continuous. Fear, if it exists, is at minimal levels. People grow together. Teachers teach and students learn. The music teacher fulfills the multi-faceted roles of program leadership.

Moving higher, effective music teachers strive to build a strong team. They empower staff assistants, student and parent leaders, and delegate effectively. They focus on developing people and surround themselves with superstars. They invest time in helping others become effective leaders. They fully realize their influence, reach out, and help others fulfill their dreams. They maintain high expectations and consistently achieve results.

The special few reach the fifth level of leadership, personhood. They understand that sustaining their work can best be accomplished by grooming a successor. Succession planning becomes a focus of their work. These are the music teachers who are held in such high regard that people assume they cannot be replaced. People are surprised when the successor, who was being quietly trained by an expert leader, makes a smooth transition. Music teachers who reach the personhood level of leadership are sought as consultants and receive numerous tributes and honors when they retire.

As Maxwell warns, don't try to skip a level. Also, the wise music teacher must never neglect the components of the lower levels. Furthermore, you must always pick an appropriate level to interact with subordinates and always know what level each has attained.

Leadership is all about influence—nothing more, nothing less. To lead music programs to higher levels, teachers must first know themselves, work to gain influence, and understand the process, pitfalls, path, and levels of leadership. Learning and gaining influence never ends.

Always work to become a better leader. Fortunately for Jose, he was guided by a caring mentor who helped him learn how to lead. Sadly, many others never do and leave the profession.

~

Invest in Professional Attire

Don't go to work dressed like you did for college classes. Look like a professional.

Nothing is more farcical than listening to a band or choir director chastise a student's lack of regard for the way they wear a uniform or present themselves for a concert when they resemble a slob. How can adults subject themselves to such silliness and absurdity?

It is generally accepted that musicians will adopt some form of professional attire for performance venues. Let's keep those standards high and work to teach students the importance looking and playing their best at all times. There are detailed expectations for orchestra members as they dress in concert black. The Marines look sharp in their dress blues. We wouldn't expect physicians to be dirty in their whites and scrubs. We dress for football games differently than to attend the symphony. Lawyers are expected to wear the classic suit. Teachers need to ratchet-up their dress code and prepare for the professional work they do.

Students might not have vivid memories of what you did or said each day, but they will be able to describe how you dressed. Look your best. Create an image. Realize the influence you have with people, especially your students, and work to leave a good impression each day.

And don't overlook the importance of personal grooming while wearing your professional attire.

Dress first-class.
Think first-class.
Act first-class.

TIP 99

~

Take Piano Lessons

Of all instruments, the piano seems to be central to more elements of music than any other. And far too many music teachers have inadequate piano skills. If you haven't studied since you were in school, it is time to find a good teacher and get back to work.

Sure, you can think of many excuses related to time or money. But you need to take care of yourself, continue learning, and grow professionally. Studying piano helps you relate with your students. You'll internalize the challenge of balancing your time and responsibilities as you find time to practice. You'll keep your fingers agile and strong. You'll reinforce your self-discipline, creativity, and thinking. Most importantly, you'll improve skills that will enhance your teaching and musicianship.

Your students will benefit from a positive example of adult learning.

TIP 100

~

Take Classes and Attend Workshops

Upgrading credentials and renewing licenses and certificates requires post-graduate work. Some state regulations require teachers to earn the equivalent of a master's degree within a specified period of time once they begin their careers. But too often, the requirements for obtaining post-graduate credits allow the substitution of continuing education units or impertinent workshops in lieu of college courses or discipline-focused workshops.

Adults learn best when their experiences are authentic and pertinent to their immediate needs. Veteran teachers will recall that their steepest learning curves likely occurred immediately out of college or when they accepted a new position. During those times, they likely sought out and relied upon their mentors for support and guidance. Enrollment in a college course or workshop could have become another alternative.

Your interest in learning and desire for knowledge should be ongoing. But you have no time to go back to campus? No time to attend workshops? Enroll for an online class or join an online professional chat group. Focus your learning around your immediate needs. You'll benefit from the synergy that emerges when bright minds share time together.

Most people regard their college experiences as one of the best periods of their lives. Never allow the memories of those times or the inspiration one gains learning with others to end. Being a continuous learner leads to better health, fewer incidents of depression, less isolation, and increased energy and motivation. If you think you are too old or no longer need to take classes, what you are really doing is showing others that you no longer have the capacity to grow and expand your horizons.

Demonstrate your ability to be a lifelong learner.

~

Be Active in State and National Associations

It is common practice that teachers annually join their state and national education associations. Increasingly, collection of membership dues can be negotiated as part of the master contract with an automatic deduction from paychecks—but not the dues for specific state and national music associations. These are often out-of-pocket expenses. But don't let that deter you. Your membership in professional music associations is worth every penny you will pay.

The support from magazines, journals, professional development offerings, state and national conventions, Web sites, liability insurance, legal updates, mailings, research, and books is vital to the growth of every music teacher. Use what is provided. Contribute and help make things even better. Share best practices. Attend professional meetings. Volunteer for committees and leadership roles. Know your colleagues. You'll find reinforcement in numbers.

Look at it another way. In every group, there are those who make things happen, participate in activities, lead, and plan and make decisions for the good of all. And then there are the nonjoiners. They are your colleagues who do just enough to get by. They cause problems and give every other music teacher a bad name. They don't grow. They isolate themselves and fail to learn best practices. They drag anchor on everyone who works hard and keeps current. And sometimes, they gain the same benefits that others worked hard to attain, but complain that conditions are bad.

Teaching music is an ever-changing job. Your professional associations are led by the best and the brightest. Join them. Be part of the group. Your involvement, ideas, and contributions will make them even better.

Self-Assessment Guide, Part VI:
Establishing and Enhancing Habits of Professional Growth

How to Use This Assessment Guide

Reflecting privately, or with the support of others, assess your current professional performance, or your preparation for the profession, along the continuum of responses provided in the chart (the numbered items correspond with the tips in the preceding section). There are no right answers; just be honest with yourself. When you are finished, your assessment might reveal needs and areas for further skill development.

You might also encourage a teacher, a friend, or a mentor to share with you how each perceives your professional work and compare and reflect together.

Informal self-assessment and evaluation are important endeavors for all professionals. If you frequently engage in reflective activities you should be well prepared for any outcomes of formal evaluation processes.

My preparation and/or professional performance skills indicate that I . . .	Strongly Disagree	Disagree	Neutral	Agree	Strongly Agree	No Opinion, No Response
79. display high levels of work efficacy and organization.						
80. respect others by promptly responding to phone calls and e-mails.						
81. deal effectively with conflict and show restraint.						
82. prepare students and myself for the future.						
83. understand the needs and desires of my constituents.						
84. avoid the habit of procrastination.						
85. act as a positive role model for students.						
86. work as a team player within the music department and school staff.						
87. understand the chain of command and show respect for superiors.						

My preparation and/or professional performance skills indicate that I . . .	Strongly Disagree	Disagree	Neutral	Agree	Strongly Agree	No Opinion, No Response
88. gain ideas and new insights by observing master teachers.						
89. guard against overextending myself.						
90. read professional books and journals and write effectively.						
91. give professional presentations.						
92. seek advice and support from a mentor.						
93. maintain a performance venue.						
94. work to improve stage presence and speaking skills.						
95. collaborate and actively network with other professionals.						
96. work to achieve levels of performance beyond the status quo.						
97. improve leadership skills.						
98. dress like a professional; think like a professional; act like a professional.						
99. engage in further studies of music; improve piano skills.						
100. attend conferences and workshops.						
101. maintain continuous membership in local, state, and national professional associations.						

~

Thanking My Music Teachers

I'm fortunate to have been taught and influenced by many people in school and my professional life. The positive lessons I've learned have shaped my work and my take on the world. I see reflections and imagine words of advice from these influential people in most everything I do. But foremost among all the dominant forces that have shaped my life are my music teachers.

I'm proud to acknowledge what I learned from those that have passed as well as those who are still a part of my life. I appreciate their constant and unforgiving encouragement and training. I owe a debt of gratitude to each of them for the specialized and artistic training that has served me well in numerous settings during more than 35 years as an educator.

My mother always knew I had a gift and was my first teacher. At an early age I showed an interest in music, eagerly participating in plays in elementary school and church. I enjoyed learning in school and achieved well in most academic areas. But it was in my music classes that I loved learning the most. I idolized Mrs. Sapp as she played the piano and led our class in singing songs. When we were introduced to the flutophone in fourth grade, my interest in instruments quickly developed. The hand-me-down trombone my parents gave me in fifth grade eventually became synonymous with my identity. Playing the trombone provided me innumerable learning opportunities outside the classroom that reinforced my confidence within.

As a principal, I strongly encouraged students and parents to become involved in the study of music, especially that of piano or any other instrument. And I was always saddened when some became discouraged and quit. I knew the value of learning music and wanted all my kids to gain that benefit. I know that sticking with something isn't easy but that perseverance can lead to huge payoffs. Many times I tried in vain to intervene and help parents envision a productive future. I wanted everyone to be able to experience what I valued. My teachers had modeled for me how to convey motivation, encouragement, and perseverance.

Today, I am a voracious reader. I can also sightread music and understand the theory and nuances of complicated musical works. I can't imagine how others experience their world without a musical and artistic perspective. Music affects my moods, my daily rhythm and intellectual insights, my interpersonal communication skills, and my understanding of the human spirit.

Music study has given me much, much more. I'm thankful that my music teachers modeled and taught me the value of:

1. Discipline: It wasn't always fun to practice while others seemed freer to play. In high school, I often had to get up early and arrive home late after performances. I learned to manage time, follow a schedule, prepare in advance for performances, and to accept disappointment. Quitting was never an option. Discipline was all about teaching and learning, not punishing, and the lessons I learned built upon each other, leading to higher levels of self-responsibility.

2. Confidence: In order to perform well, I had to practice. Once I could play a difficult passage 10 times without error, the challenge became routine and almost automatic. This skill became an asset when it became time to teach difficult concepts or speak in front of large audiences. I practiced what I wanted to say and teach until I knew it by memory.

3. High expectations: Speaking with incorrect grammar is like playing wrong notes. Playing wrong notes has never been acceptable. My music teachers always expected me to perform at my best. So a strong work ethic became an asset more important than skill or talent. It remains one of my strongest characteristics.

4. Performance: As a teacher, my classroom was a stage and I was the actor. Experience in front of people and the ability to perform helped me become an effective public speaker—an essential skill for teachers, and especially for principals.

5. Competition: I was fortunate to participate with several other good trombone players in my high school band. We pushed each other. We strove to be the best. We learned to compete against individual abilities as with each other. We remain friends today. And when consider-

ing the entire ensemble, our director was never satisfied with second place. He never shied away from competing with other bands. He made sure our training and shows were second to none. Competition drives our world. Those who can compete—and have learned to do so fairly—will surely have advantage over those who can't.

6. Teamwork: Take away the vowels *u* and *i* from the word music and you're left with ineffective consonants. Performing as a duet or with more people in a larger ensemble requires give and take between you and me. For the team to work, I have to be able to do my part. So do you and numerous others. When participants in an ensemble can't work as a team, their results are ineffective.

7. Socialization: In my bands, there were always many talented players but many that were not. We accepted all kinds. Kids came from all socioeconomic groups and backgrounds. Each learned to get along with the other and work together for a common good. Each knew the pride that came from being part of the band. The band experience was a key to making the high school years memorable for many students.

8. Aesthetics: Many people waste much of their leisure time. They don't understand or appreciate the finer things of life. All teachers have a responsibility to expose their students to what is best in life. My music teachers introduced me to aesthetic beauty and enabled me to create it for myself through my expression of art.

9. Creativity: Research shows that creative artists more dominantly utilize the right side of the brains. Today's schools need leaders with fresh ideas who can ingenuously solve problems and continuously improve.

10. Geography: My high school musical experiences enabled me to travel throughout my state. Since then, music-related endeavors have provided me reasons and opportunities to travel the world. I studied maps and witnessed firsthand the marvels and uniqueness of places around the globe. I might have gained less appreciation for other cultures had my music teachers not understood the importance of travel.

11. Connectedness: I have been able to communicate and perform with people from other countries that did not speak my language because we connected through music. An F-sharp is *sol* in every language. Language and communication are all about expressing human thought and emotion. Music possesses that capacity and power in universal ways.

12. History: People have expressed themselves through their music since the beginning of time. My most enjoyable history lessons, which

remain stuck in my memory, were those that were taught from the musical perspective in the form of a story about a composer, performer, or musical practices of another time. My music teachers were knowledgeable, enthusiastic historians. When they talked about the music of composers of the Renaissance or the Romantic eras, it was as if they knew them on a familiar basis. They taught our U.S. heritage through musicals, a study of jazz, and many other popular genres that have influenced and shaped the modern world. For many students today, the study of history would be more meaningful if music were a major component of the curriculum.

13. Religion: It's unlikely that you'll study the religions of the world without understanding the influence of music and the key role that the master composers played in expressing their pious thoughts and those of others through their art. History comes alive when experiencing the classic works. Music, more than any other art form, is a critical component of most religious liturgical practices. Since before the Reformation, composers and believers have recognized its power in touching the innermost human soul.

14. Math: Looking back on my learning experiences in elementary school, I can't recall which I learned first—concepts of fractions or the relationship of whole, half, quarter, and eighth notes. Certainly, learning the values of notes and rests and their theoretical relationship reinforced my math skills, particularly when master teachers helped us all understand and apply what we learned. Effective teachers have always done this. And those who have studied music are often among the most effective.

15. Physical education: When I taught music, many of my marching band participants were as fit as any athlete in our school. Our rehearsals included a running regimen that built stamina and endurance for parades and performances. We were conscious of our weight and worked to control it. Not surprising, many former students have maintained fitness habits as adults. Now nearing age 60, I still look forward to jogging and enjoy many of the good health benefits that are associated with it. I often contemplate what my life would be like had I not been conditioned and trained during a time when a high step marching style and perpetual motion were definitive components of a marching band.

16. Football: My two brothers were the football players of the family. In contrast, I didn't care to get dirty or hurt. But as a member of my high school marching band, I grew to understand the game and became an avid fan. Moreover, I grew to appreciate and value the important role I played contributing to and influencing the pageantry of high

school and college football. I learned to appreciate the skills and commitment of coaches and their players and the important identity that football brings to a community. My band director was a football enthusiast and a good role model for what can be positive about music and athletics teaming and cooperation.

17. Coordination: I marvel at the advanced levels of coordination displayed by those football players who catch the clutch passes. I credit their abilities to talent and excellent coaching. But I was also quick to inform those coaches that my majorettes displayed as many or more skills when they caught their baton under a leg in a short skirt in subfreezing temperatures after tossing that cold metallic object high in the air while at the same time completing several complete body turns while smiling, all to the exact beat of the music being played by others and echoing throughout the stadium. And I also let the girls know they had nobody else to blame if they dropped it—no quarterback could blame others for a bad pass. There is also nothing more amazing than an organist who can use all 10 fingers on two or more different keyboards while at the same time using both feet on the foot pedals—playing polyrhythmic works by avant-garde composers.

18. Self-esteem: Because I showed no interest in playing football, music became a means that my parents and music teachers used to build my self-esteem. I may not have always performed well, but they always had encouraging words. For a few moments, I was the center of attention, the star on the stage. Later, as my self-confidence grew, the critiques from my music teachers became more honest, but always with sincerity and a sense of caring. I always had people encouraging me and validating what I did. The same is true for countless others who study music.

19. Vocation: For me, music is more than a vocation. It became a basis upon which I established a career. Experiencing music has become a way of life for me and my family. But for millions of others, it is more a vocation, an enjoyable and enriching part of life. My music teachers helped all their students appreciate music and discover ways that it could influence the quality of their lives—in many ways other than performance. They helped us become knowledgeable consumers, one of the most enduring gifts we received from our school experience.

20. Organization: It only took one bad experience of forgetting my instrument and part of my uniform to learn better organizational skills. Because of the lessons I learned in band, I can manage time effectively, pack a suitcase without forgetting necessary items, know the location of my possessions, and complete tasks on time. These and many other skills like them are important for success in the workplace.

21. Commitment: Participation in a marching band requires a total commitment of time and effort. It is the same for any music performing group. My family shared and encouraged my commitment, both as a youngster and a teacher. We shared common goals, joys and disappointments. Most of all, we shared time. Together, we arranged our family schedule and worked to fulfill all obligations. That left little time to stray and get into trouble. To misstep would have led to embarrassment and inability to fulfill my commitment.

22. Independence: As I progressed on the trombone, the more motivated I became to learn how to play other instruments and to become a better singer. I taught myself how to play the tuba, trumpet, and French horn. My teachers encouraged me and modeled adult learning at all times. In our music classes, we were taught to accept responsibility for our learning, to help and learn from each other, and correct the teachers when they made errors. Most of all, we were taught that if we wanted to succeed at whatever challenges we chose to undertake, we had to accept responsibility and learn for ourselves, at all times, especially outside the classroom and the school.

23. Resiliency: My bands placed first in their class at many contests. Individuals often achieved superior ratings in solo and ensemble contests. But they also came up short on many occasions. Like my teachers did for me and my peers, I tried to be there to nurture them through the agony of defeat. Most learned to shake off adversity and work for improvement that would lead to success at another time. That lesson, which I learned from my music teachers, prepared me for hard knocks in my career in teaching and also the challenges of rearing two daughters. When we were beaten, or knocked down, we were taught to reflect and learn from our mistakes, show resolve, and get back up and move forward for future opportunities. This lesson, as much as any other, served me well in the political world of school administration.

24. Respect: Part of learning music is listening to others. I learned to respect the accomplishments of others and to express that sentiment in an appropriate manner. I learned to listen to those who were older and to defer to their opinions. To be admired by others was to aspire to what they also accomplished. It was a standard declaration that the seniors ruled. We were taught to hold their accomplishments in high esteem.

25. Punctuality: If rehearsals were scheduled to begin at 2:00, I learned never to be late. So did my students. Being on time was easier than

enduring my scorn for being tardy. No matter what was happening, we were taught to hustle and be ready to rehearse or perform at a designated time. We were taught that it was inconsiderate and rude to be late and keep others from being able to start a rehearsal. Today, I am driven by the clock, dislike being late for anything, and expect those who work with me to respect the virtue of punctuality.

26. Communication: Effective music teachers are good communicators. They know and value the importance of keeping parents aware of expectations, schedules, goals, and progress. They also learn to speak confidently in front of large audiences. They use correct grammar. They are motivators. They are persuasive. They serve as role models for their students.

27. Sense of community: For the students in my band, we became a community of learners within our high school. We shared interests, turf, time, and resources. We shared our identity. We became a source of pride within the school, and our community rallied around the band and likewise shared our identity. Often, when outsiders heard the name of our school, they first connected what they knew about our band. I learned, and so did my students, the sense of pride that comes from contributing to our community's identity. This is a valuable lesson, worth more than money. It is one that I tried to convey and build within each school while a principal.

28. Risk-taking: My teachers always encouraged and pushed me to try a piece of music that pushed me out of my comfort zone. They stressed the importance of taking risks and accepting challenges that others would shy away from. My music teachers taught me to do rather than watching others, lead instead of following. The self-confidence and disregard of fear that developed from these lessons enabled me to motivate and encourage others to follow me and remove obstacles that others often could not.

29. Dress code: Prior to any performance of my marching bands, my students and I conducted a uniform inspection. The kids spent hours paying close attention to the smallest details of their appearance. They took pride in how they looked and were proud of the uniform they wore. I believe it is very important to look your best. I hold firmly to the belief that professional people distinguish themselves when they dress first class, think first class, and act first class.

30. Mentoring: My relationship with my music teachers was much more than teacher-student. We became close. Some became pseudo-parents. They scolded me when I deserved it. Other times they

showered me with praise. We shared personal interests. We taught each other. We shared confidences. We became a team. Besides teaching me all they knew about music, but they also provided direction in any other aspect of my learning and growth that they thought would help me. They taught the whole learner. They guided, nurtured, coached, and loved. They taught me how to live and love life. They paid forward, and I can never thank them enough.

Summary

Some extremely talented, virtuosic musicians become prima donnas. But elementary music teachers, generally, are often overlooked among the superstars in their profession. That is not to say they don't have egos because to teach and perform they must. My earliest music teachers were not very concerned about the spotlight. They were in love with their art and committed to sharing it with others around then, especially their students. They were patient and nurturing. Then in high school and college, I encountered music teachers that were very influential with commanding personalities. They demanded that my peers and I achieve at high levels and with skills we didn't know we possessed. They had a vision of what we could become and helped shape us in numerous ways to become better musicians and successful adults. All my music teachers were among the best of the superstars!

Unfortunately, music teaching positions are sometimes among those first to be eliminated when school budget crises develop. Some school administrators justify these actions citing that music isn't a core part of the basic course of study. In an attempt to assure that all students achieve high standards as measured by high-stakes tests, resources are directed toward reading, math, science, and test preparation. That practice is folly. The kids who would benefit most from the study of music are those most likely to miss out. Without a doubt, when music classes are cut, at-risk students miss opportunities to become hooked in by the subject that will provide reasons for them to come to school. Music, more than any other part of the curriculum, unlocks the mind and builds connections with all the other subjects providing lessons and positive outcomes that stick with learners through life.

I was one of those who got hooked in. As a result, I loved school. As a teacher, I was passionate about teaching a subject I loved and experienced a fulfilling career. My success and happiness was made possible by my music teachers.

I humbly thank them all.

~

Coda

Before I finish, allow me to extemporize just a little more . . .

If you were to ask kids the question "Do you like classical music?" far too many might answer, "No, it stinks!" or "It's dull and boring!" Most have little experience upon which to base their response. Unlike pop, rock, or rap music that is immediately accessible to young people via CDs, DVDs, iPods, MTV, television, radio, and other media, classical music is heard mostly in elevators or the doctor's office. As increasing numbers of students go through school without experiencing and understanding classical music; the performing arts are becoming ever more exclusive, enjoyed and appreciated by a dwindling educated elite. Who and what are to blame? Many answers can be theorized. But clearly a group with direct influence, good or bad, are the thousands of public school music educators in our nation's schools.

Why study classical music? Why any art form? The arts teach the learner to appreciate aesthetics, communicate across cultures, and create a sense of identity and special being. The arts help learners to imagine, create, and make sense of the world in ways that areas of the curricula cannot. The fine arts are a key part of what makes a person well educated. They enlighten and fulfill the emotional and spiritual well-being. Understanding the arts enables one to comprehend and interpret the complexities of the world's mysteries. Learning how to listen to classical music enables listeners to appreciate the finest achievements of mankind.

A majority of the nation's orchestras, which represent the "highest culture" in many urban areas, are in desperate financial trouble. Failure over

time to produce learned, appreciative generations of classical music con-
noisseurs is resulting in fewer corporate sponsors, wealthy benefactors, and
donors. Likewise, music teachers in the specialty areas, such as orchestra and
composition, have become a frill and cut in many districts due to budgetary
restrictions. How long until music education is no longer valued for even the
most basic, required courses of study?

Still unaffected by the changes around them, too many public school music educators are content with the status quo. They focus their attention on
performing groups, and on those students who show the most promise. They
exclude students who lack the means to acquire a quality instrument, progress rapidly, or pursue private study. They cater to the most affluent parents
whose children have access to the best opportunities. They fail to establish
and affirm music education as an indispensable part of the general curriculum
for *all* students.

Attitudes must change. Expensive music programs (and teachers) are
too costly to maintain with fewer numbers of participants. Teachers must
develop inclusive attitudes, recruit and retain the interest of participants,
and rely less on the outcomes of performance groups to justify their programs. Replicating conventional programs is no longer satisfactory. Music
programs must become innovative and experimental. They must be revital-
ized, and the curriculum must be structured in ways that pass on our culture
through comprehensive lessons in music history, aesthetics, creating music,
and integrating the arts into the everyday world. All students must have opportunities to learn to read music, utilize music technology, and appreciate
the civilizing force of the arts. They must do more than perform. Failure to
change will lead to the demise of public school music programs, leaving, if
any, only the most basic music courses. The arts will be left to those fortunate
enough to afford the exclusive opportunities of the private sector.

Music teachers must understand that their most important goal is to continually create new audiences among the masses. The study of music must be
for all. With that realization, music educators must unite their efforts to instill deeper meaning, understanding, and public purpose into their programs,
increase their status and value within the school system, while creating a
brighter future for a trained, supportive public.

> The future belongs to a very different kind of person with a very differ-
> ent kind of mind—creators and empathizers, pattern recognizers, and
> meaning makers. These people—artists, inventors, designers, storytell-
> ers, caregivers, consolers, big picture thinkers—will now reap society's
> richest rewards and its greatest joys.
>
> —Daniel Pink, author of *A Whole New Mind*

~

References and
Recommended Readings

Bakke, D. W. (2005). *Joy at work*. Seattle: PVG.

Barrett, J. (2005). Teaching a la cart: Music on wheels. *Teaching Music*, 12(5), 28–32.

Blaydes, J. (2003). *The educator's book of quotes*. Thousand Oaks, CA: Corwin Press.

Clark, R. (2004). *The excellent 11: Qualities teachers and parents use to motivate, inspire, and educate children*. New York: Hyperion.

Colvin, G. (2008). *Talent is overrated: What really separates world-class performers from everybody else*. New York: Penguin Group.

Core Knowledge Foundation. (1998). *Core knowledge sequence*. Charlottesville, VA: Core Knowledge Foundation.

Deasy, R. J., ed. (2002). *Critical links*. Washington, DC: Arts Education Partnership.

Fowler, C. (1996). *Strong arts, strong schools*. New York: Oxford University Press.

Fox, J. J. (2001). *How to land your dream job*. New York: Hyperion.

Fullen, M. (2008). *The six secrets of change*. San Francisco: Jossey-Bass.

Fulton, R. (1995). *Common sense leadership*. Berkeley: Ten Speed Press.

Gardner, H. (1983). *Frames of mind: The theory of multiple intelligences*. New York: Basic Books.

Gardner, H. (2006). *Five minds for the future*. Boston: Harvard Business School Press.

Gladwell, M. (2008). *Outliers*. New York: Little, Brown, & Company.

Hansen, M. V., & Batten, J. (1995). *The master motivator*. New York: Barnes and Noble Books.

Jones, R. *Tips for music teachers*. Retrieved February 12, 2008, fromwww.mtrs.co.uk/tips.htm.

Kosmoski, G. J., & Pollack, D. R. (2000). *Managing difficult, frustrating, and hostile conversations*. Thousand Oaks, CA: Corwin Press, Inc.

Labuta, J. A., & Smith, D. A. (1997). *Music education: Historical contexts and perspectives*. Upper Saddle River, NJ: Prentice-Hall, Inc.

Lee, C. (2004). *Preventing bullying in schools*. London: Paul Chapman Publishing.

Lehman, P. (1988). What students should learn in the arts. *Content of the Curriculum, ASCD Yearbook*, 109–131.

Lencioni, P. (2007). *Three signs of a miserable job*. San Francisco: Jossey-Bass.

Levitin, D. J. (2006). *This is your brain on music*. New York: Penguin Group.

Marzano, R. J. (2003). *Classroom management that works*. Alexandria, VA: Association for Curriculum and Development.

Maxwell, J. C. (2002). *Leadership 101*. Nashville: Thomas Nelson Publishers.

Maxwell, J. C. (2003). *Attitude 101*. Nashville: Thomas Nelson Publishers.

Maxwell, J. C. (2003). *Ethics 101*. Nashville: Thomas Nelson Publishers.

Maxwell, J. C. (2007). *Be a people person*. Colorado Springs: David C. Cook.

McKain, S. (2002). *All business is show business*. Nashville: Rutledge Hill Press.

McKenna, C. (1998). *Powerful communication skills: How to communicate with confidence*. New York: Barnes & Noble Books.

Music Educators National Conference. (2004). *Teacher to teacher: A music educator's survival guide*. Reston, VA: Music Educators National Conference.

Music Educators National Conference. (2005). *Careers in music*. Retrieved February 12, 2008, from www.menc.org/information/infoserv/careersinmusic.htm.

Music Educators National Conference. (2005). *National standards for music education*. Retrieved February 28, 2005, fromwww.menc.org/publication/books/standards.htm [now www.menc.org/resources/view/national-standards-for-music-education].

Ohio Department of Education. (2004). *Academic content standards, K–12 fine arts*. Columbus: Ohio Department of Education Center for Curriculum and Assessment.

Payne, R. K. (2005). *A framework for understanding poverty*. Highlands, TX: aha!Process, Inc.

Payne, R. K., Devol, P. E., & Smith, T. D. (2006). *Bridges out of poverty: Strategies for professionals and communities*. Highlands, TX: aha!Process, Inc.

Pink, D. H. (2005). *A whole new mind*. New York: Riverhead Books, Penguin Group.

Raessler, K. R. (2003). *Aspiring to excellence: Leadership initiatives for music educators*. Chicago: GIA Publications, Inc.

Rudney, G. L., & Guillaume, A. M. (2003). *Maximum mentoring: An action guide for teacher trainers and cooperating teachers*. Thousand Oaks, CA: Corwin Press.

Sanborn, M. (2006). *You don't need a title to be a leader*. New York: Doubleday.

Schellenberg, E. G. (2004). Music lessons enhance IQ. *Psychological Science, 12*(8), 511–514.

Singer, E. (2004). Molecular basis for Mozart effect revealed. Retrieved March 16, 2005, from www.newscientist.com/article.ns?id=dn4918.

Whitaker, T., & Lumpa, D. (2005). *Great quotes from great educators*. Larchmont, NY: Eye on Education.

Young, P. G. (2004). *You have to go to school—You're the principal: 101 tips to make it better for your students, your staff, and yourself*. Thousand Oaks, CA: Corwin Press.

Young, P. G. (2008). *Promoting positive behaviors: An elementary principal's guide to structuring the learning environment*. Thousand Oaks, CA: Corwin Press.

~

About the Author

Paul Young, Ph.D., is the Executive Director of the West After School Center in Lancaster, Ohio. He began his career as a high school band director and then taught fourth and fifth grades before advancing to an elementary principalship in 1986.

He served as president of the Ohio Association of Elementary School Administrators (OAESA) in 1997 and was elected to the National Association of Elementary School Principals (NAESP) board of directors in 1998 (the only person elected by write-in ballot). He became president-elect in 2001–2002 and served as the national president during the 2002–2003 school year. He retired from the principalship in December 2004. Currently, he is a member of the board of directors of the National After School Association.

Additionally, Young has taught undergraduate music classes at Ohio University–Lancaster for more than 25 years. He continues to teach private trombone lessons. He is a strong advocate for the arts. He believes that there is a strong correlation with school quality and the number of students involved in high school music programs. He has initiated opportunities for underprivileged students to further develop their interests in vocal and instrumental music at the West After School Center.

He completed a Bachelor of Fine Arts in music education in 1972 and a Master of Music in trombone performance in 1973, both from Ohio University–Athens. He earned a Ph.D. in educational administration from Ohio University in 1992. He is the past president of the Ohio University School of Music Society of Alumni and Friends.

His wife Gertrude also has completed Bachelor of Fine Arts and Master of Music degrees from Ohio University. She is a vocal and instrumental music teacher in the Lancaster City Schools. Daughter Katie is the principal oboist with the Florida Orchestra in Tampa. She earned music education degrees and performance certificates from the Eastman School of Music and Rice University. Daughter Mary Ellen is a graduate of the University of Cincinnati College of Business. She studied piano and French horn. She is a sales representative for McGraw-Hill Higher Education/Humanities. She and her husband, Eric Rahn, live in Chicago and are avid music lovers and supporters.

Young is the author of *Mastering the Art of Mentoring Principals; You Have to Go to School, You're the Principal!: 101 Tips to Make it Better for Your Students, Your Staff, and Yourself; Mentoring Principals: Frameworks, Agendas, Tips, and Case Studies for Mentors and Mentees; Promoting Positive Behaviors: An Elementary Principal's Guide to Structuring the Learning Environment;* and *Principal Matters: 101 Tips for Creating Collaborative Relationships Between After-School Programs and School Leaders.* He has also written numerous articles about music, the arts, after-school programming, and the principalship for professional journals.

Breinigsville, PA USA
22 September 2010
245800BV00006B/3/P